Spanish that Works

...for You

A creative, functional approach to basic communication in Spanish

Elizabeth Almann, Author
Alexander Almann, Illustrations

 The Learning Light
Educational Materials & Service

 Bee Bilingual!

Spanish that Works for You (revised edition)

An original publication of The Learning Light, LLC.
Billings, Montana, USA. Printed by Lightning Source.

The Learning Light
Educational Materials & Service

Elizabeth Almann, Author
Alexander Almann, Illustrations
Jacqueline DiMascio, Cover Design
Margaret Thompson, Patricia Boschini, James W. Thompson,
Dr. John P. Thompson, and Patricia Rocha, Editing

Special thanks to Teton County Library, SonRise Faith Community Center,
City of Mesa Public Library and City Court, Scottsdale Unified School District,
and to all my students who told me what they wanted to know.

For group copy licensing information or for teacher resources,
visit: **http://www.thelearninglight.com (www.spanishthatworks.org)**
call toll free: **1-866-391-8901**
or write to:

The Learning Light, LLC
333 Lewis Avenue, Billings, MT, 59101 USA

Bee Bilingual!   Spanish that Works

Bee Bilingual! **and** *Spanish that Works*
are trademarks of The Learning Light, LLC

Thank you for supporting *Spanish that Works!*

ISBN #978-0-9744476-7-4

Preface to the Student

¡Bienvenido! ¡Bienvenida! (Welcome!)

Welcome to *Spanish that Works!* You are about to embark upon an exciting and fun adventure: learning how to **speak** another language.

This course was written to give you a working knowledge of practical Spanish, so that you can communicate better with others in your community or at work. Perhaps this is your first time studying Spanish, or perhaps you have taken Spanish before and you just want a refresher.

Whatever your background or situation, the following suggestions will help you to make *Spanish that Works* work for you.

Steps to a Successful Experience

Know your Materials

Spanish that Works for You is comprised of eight units (sixteen lessons) and a supplemental section. Each lesson requires at least an hour of initial study. The amount of time needed to become comfortable with the material depends on the learner, but for most people, one additional hour per lesson is a good start.

Materials to enrich your learning experience, including downloadable reference sheets and cut-out flashcard pages (some for free), are available online at **www.spanishthatworks.org (www.thelearninglight.com)**.

Also available via the website are: an audio program with the basic vocabulary, a distance-learning video series of the course done live-to-tape for community television, specialty vocabulary modules, a teacher's guide and other instructor resources, supplemental lessons, and recommendations for further study.

Follow the Rules

Although *Spanish that Works* does not emphasize grammatical rules and structures, the speaking exercises produce good results when you follow the method outlined in the course. The *Spanish that Works for You* text workbook has information about how to use the pronunciation guide, flashcards, mini-dialogues, and sentence builders, which are all key components of the *Spanish that Works* method.

Ideally, you will be using these materials in class with a *Spanish that Works* teacher. Part of the success of the method comes from the interactive practice with other students and the feedback from the instructor. If you are working on your own, or to get additional pointers for studying at home, read the "Guidelines for Learning on Your Own" on pages S-4 and S-5 of the supplemental section.

Have Patience and Dedication

Learning a new language takes time, and fluency will build gradually, so be patient with yourself. If you don't "get" it, you just need more practice. In this course, you will **repeat, repeat, repeat** until you are comfortable, so just concentrate on the task at hand and know that eventually you will succeed.

Study a little bit each day, even if it's just ten or fifteen minutes with your flashcards or the audio program. If you are in a class, you may want to read ahead so you are familiar with the material before it is formally introduced. The more times you go over your vocabulary words, the more Spanish will make sense, and seem natural to you.

Also, listen to Spanish as much as possible. Interact with native speakers or others who are learning, or watch movies or television in Spanish. It doesn't matter if you don't understand every word—just get used to the sounds.

A great way to train your ear and to pick up new words is to listen to music in Spanish. For recommendations, visit our website: **www.spanishthatworks.org** or check out your local library or bookstore.

Keep a Sense of Humor

Don't worry about having to know or understand everything, or about "getting it right." Mistakes and misunderstandings are part of the fun of language. Think about it—a lot of humor is based on confused or double-meanings, so if there were no misunderstandings, we wouldn't have as many jokes.

It's helpful to think of funny ways to remember new words. For example the word **allá** / ah-YAH, which means "over there," sounds like a karate chop yell (hi-YAH!). Imagine someone karate chopping a board, which flies way OVER THERE (hi-YAH, ah-YAH!). Creative word associations will help you to learn vocabulary.

Remember to laugh. You want to take your learning seriously, but you don't want to take yourself too seriously.

Follow the Pronunciation Guide

Spanish is a different language, so you can't read it like English.

The pronunciation guide in this course is written for American English speakers, and is designed to help you approximate the sounds of Spanish. Just read the guide as an English nonsense word. It looks strange, but it works!

The guide won't make sense to non-native English speakers, so don't expect Spanish speakers to understand it. And if you are not a native speaker of English, you may have to make some adjustments to the guide, especially for the R and D.

If you have difficulties with a Spanish word, it's probably because English is getting in the way. If this is the case, cross out the Spanish spelling and learn the word from the pronunciation guide ONLY. This is a speaking course, so it's more important that you know how to say the words than how to spell them. Once you can say the words, the spelling is easy.

It will be helpful to ask someone who has native pronunciation of Spanish to listen to you as you pronounce the words, and give constructive feedback. This is especially important if you are learning on your own.

 *Bee Bilingual!*

Think in Spanish

This course is different from traditional language teaching methods. You won't conjugate verbs or read and answer questions. Instead, you'll learn Spanish with flashcards and mini-dialogues which prepare you to **speak** the language in situations that can occur in real life.

Follow the rules for practicing the mini-dialogues as outlined in Lesson Two. The idea is to repeat each dialogue over and over with different vocabulary words. Don't skip around or try to improvise, because you will be translating from English. Just follow the pattern. When the pattern becomes "natural," you will be able to say what you want without having to think about it. This is where true fluency comes from.

Learn by Example, not by Rule

Spanish that Works focuses on teaching the example, rather than the rule.

Grammar rules help you understand why something is said or to edit something you've written, but it takes too much time to try to remember rules when you are in a speaking situation.

For this reason, it is better to learn phrases that express the rules in context. For example, rather than learning all the rules and variations for **está** and **es** (both mean "is"), learn to say **¿Dónde está...?** (Where is...?) and **La clase es mañana** (Class is tomorrow) as complete patterns. Then you will be able to express yourself in conversation without thinking about the rules for when to use **está** and **es**.

Keep it Simple

In order to speak, work with smaller amounts of information. Think of your mind like a computer. The bigger the file, the longer it takes to "download," and in conversation you don't have time to wait.

Make your point in as few words as possible. If you can express yourself without using a verb, do it.

For example, don't use a complete sentence if it's not required. In traditional language classes, they make you answer in a complete sentence in order to get you to practice verb conjugations and other grammar. This is unnecessary and artificial for speaking.

Compare these two conversations:

<u>Traditional class</u>	<u>Natural, easy way to speak</u>
"What is your name?"	"What's your name?"
"My name is Mary."	"Mary. And you...?"
(Great for verbs and vocabulary)	(Real, effective communication)

Just focus on the key words you need, and it will be easier for you to communicate. If you try to translate complicated things from English, you may come up with structures that make no sense.

For example, you can't translate "Can I please have a juice?" with the verb **tener** (to have), because **tener** also means "to hold onto" or "to keep." You don't want to **hold onto** the juice; you just want to drink it. In Spanish, you would say something like **¿Me da un jugo?**/meh thah oon HOO-goh? (Will you give me a juice?).

Rather than saying, "Can I please have a juice?" it would be easier and more correct to say, "A juice, please" (**Un jugo, por favor**). So remember:

Simple is better, Simple is faster, Simple is more fun!

Keep an Open Mind

Learning a language is like taking a leap of faith. There will be certain English "habits" that you will need to break. If you are in a class, your teacher will be speaking Spanish as much as possible when it's not critical that you understand every word. This will be easy or difficult for you, depending on your emotional attachment to how English is structured and your willingness to try something that feels strange.

Language gives you power over your environment, and not having that power can be uncomfortable. To be successful, you must believe in what you are learning and trust that it will make sense eventually. It's not a question of being "wrong" or "right"; it's about accepting differences and seeing the beauty in a new way of talking about the world.

Find Your Own Path

This course will lead you through basic Spanish step by step. All you ever need to know will be right in front of you. So don't worry about the things you aren't learning. Just concentrate on what you are working on right now.

Look through the course text and check out **www.spanishthatworks.org** for extra materials and course updates. If there is something that you think you need to know right away, start learning it. Or, you can wait until you get to that point in the course. The journey is yours, so you are free to find your own path.

Set a Positive Intent

Positive intent is the key to having a good experience. Know that you can learn this, given enough time and practice. See yourself speaking Spanish and having fun. Think of it as a wild adventure, and enjoy the ride. You will be amazed at the results.

We hope you love this course, and love Spanish.

Spanish that Works
...for You

UNIT THREE: "Where is it? It's over there!"

UNIT FOUR: "My friend needs a pen or a pencil."

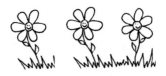

UNIT FIVE: "I'm a student. I speak a little Spanish."

UNIT SIX: "Do you want to speak Spanish?"

UNIT SEVEN: "The meeting is May 20th at 7:00 p.m."

UNIT EIGHT: "How may I help you?"

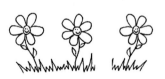

SUPPLEMENTAL SECTION: "You speak Spanish very well!"

More Information

Visit www.spanishthatworks.org for information about:
- ❖ Audio Program
- ❖ Pull-out reference sheets, flashcards, & sentence builders
- ❖ Specialty vocabulary for certain areas

UNIT ONE:

"Your name, please."

Lesson 1: Saying & Understanding

- ❖ Introduction
- ❖ Saying & Understanding Chart
- ❖ 5 Indispensable Vowels
- ❖ Challenging Consonants
- ❖ Stress & Accent Marks
- ❖ Expressions (Hi, good morning...)
- ❖ Mini-Dialogues

Lesson 2: Things

- ❖ Basic Things
- ❖ Specialty Things
- ❖ How to Practice Vocabulary
- ❖ Expressions (Please, thanks, one moment...)
- ❖ How to Use the Mini-Dialogues
- ❖ Mini-Dialogues

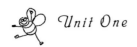

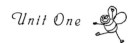

LESSON ONE: Saying & Understanding

Introduction

Contrary to what you may think, much of Spanish is pronounced similarly to English, and the letters that are different have approximate English equivalents, so it's relatively easy for an English speaker to produce Spanish sounds. The real challenge is to retrain yourself to say new sounds for letters that look like English, but sound different from what you're used to. You must learn these letters as though you were learning to read for the first time.

A good, understandable pronunciation is crucial, especially when you have little vocabulary. Your knowledge of letter-sound relationships in Spanish affects not only how others understand you, but also how you understand others when they are speaking. It may take some effort to "relearn" the alphabet, but it is essential to your success.

The pronunciation guide in this course represents the most approximate American English equivalents to Latin American Spanish sounds. If you are <u>not</u> a native speaker of American English, you may want to change the guide to be more compatible with your language. Also, the words in the guide are divided into the letter groupings that are the *easiest to follow* for an English speaker, so don't expect the guide to be an accurate representation of Spanish syllables. Native Spanish speakers may not understand the guide, but it <u>does</u> work.

You read the words in the guide as if they were *English nonsense words*. The words in the guide may seem strange, but this is because Spanish letters often represent sounds very different from English.

Since the purpose of this course is basic communication, the guide teaches only those letters that are significantly different from English. The letters are organized by sound, rather than in alphabetical order, and are taught by sound, rather than by name. There is a chart with the Spanish alphabet on page S-10 of the supplemental section, in case you ever need to spell something aloud.

Unlike English, Spanish pronunciation always matches spelling. Once you have mastered Spanish letter-sound relationships, you will be able to pronounce anything you read.

Saying & Understanding Chart

This is the information you will need to begin pronouncing Spanish. You may wish to make a copy of this chart to use as a reference sheet.

WHEN YOU SEE	YOU SAY
a	ah
e	eh (close to English "A")
i	ee
o	oh
u	oo (silent after q & g)
a, e, o in vowel combo	separate syllable
i in vowel combo	y
u in vowel combo	w
d	th of "brother" & "this"
r between vowels	fast dd of "buddy"
rr (& start/end r)	trill (dder of "ladder")
t	t of "Tom," tongue behind teeth
ll (not l)	y
ñ (not n)	ny of "canyon"
h	silent, so ignore it
j	h
g(e), g(i)	h
g(a), gu(e), gu(i). g(o), g(u)	g as in "go"
b / v	b or v, interchangeable
qu	k
z	s
word ends in vowel,-s, or -n	stress 2nd to last syllable
word ends in consonant	stress last syllable
accent mark (á, é, í, ó, ú)	stress vowel with accent

FIVE INDISPENSABLE VOWELS

Spanish has five basic vowels. **Say every single vowel you see, except for u after q or g.** **Clase** (class) has two syllables: **cla / CLAH** and **se / seh.** Except for "u" in "qu" and "gu," there are no silent vowels, or vowels that completely change when paired. **Lea** (Read!) also has two syllables: **le / LEH** and **a / ah.**

WHEN YOU SEE	YOU SAY	IT MEANS
a	**ah** (<u>never</u> "A")	letter a
a	AH	to
e	**eh** (like Canadian "eh?") (close to "A")	letter e
me	MEH (close to "may")	to me, myself
i	**ee** (close to "E")	letter i
mi	MEE	my
o	**oh** (<u>never</u> "ah")	letter o
con	COHN	with
u	**oo** (<u>never</u> "yoo")	letter u
su	SOO	Your, his, her, their

WHEN YOU SEE	SAY	IT MEANS
casa	CAH-sah	house
clase	CLAH-seh	class
¿Cómo?	COH-moh?	How?
minuto	mee-NOO-<u>t</u>oh	minute
oficina	oh-fee-SEE-nah	office
un momento	oon moh-MEHN-<u>t</u>oh	one moment
No sé.	noh SEH (SAY)	I don't know.

NOTE: Stress the syllable written in capital letters.

VOWELS IN COMBINATION

The five basic Spanish vowels may appear alone in a syllable or in combination with other vowels.

The "round" vowels "a," "e" and "o" are strong. They make up their own syllable, so if you have two of the round vowels together, you say each one, separately.

**Whenever you see "a," "e" and "o" in combinations,
think "separate syllables."**

WHEN YOU SEE	SAY	IT MEANS
leer	leh-AI*RR* (lay-AI*RR*)	to read
o sea	oh-SEH-ah (oh-SAY-ah)	or rather, I mean

The "line" vowels "i" and "u" are weak. They will blend with other vowels, unless supported by a written accent mark. You still say them; it's just so fast they get blurred. The "i" then sounds like a "y" and the "u" turns into a "w."

Whenever you see "i" in vowel combinations, think "y."

WHEN YOU SEE	SAY	IT MEANS
familia	fah-MEEL-yah	family
bien	b'YEHN	well, doing fine
patio	PAH-<u>t</u>'yoh	patio

baile	BY-leh	dance (noun)
veinte	VANE-<u>t</u>eh	twenty

Whenever you see "u" in combinations, think "w."
(Exception: "u" is silent after "q" and "g.")

WHEN YOU SEE	SAY	IT MEANS
bueno	BWEH-noh	good, nice
pues...	PWEHss	well...so...then
¿Cuánto?	KWAHN-<u>t</u>oh?	How much?

auto	OW-<u>t</u>oh ("ow" of **cow**)	auto

CHALLENGING CONSONANTS

If you have taken a Spanish class that did not teach pronunciation or are self-taught, some of the pronunciation guidelines taught here may seem strange to you, or you may believe that an English pronunciation will be adequate.

The truth is that it is not only more difficult for a Spanish speaker to understand you if you mispronounce words, but you will also have difficulty understanding spoken Spanish, because the words will NEVER sound as you expected. The next three letters are probably the most challenging consonants for English speakers to both say and understand correctly.

THE TRICKY THREE: D, R, and T

D

Unlike the English "d," the Spanish "d" is pronounced with the tongue between the teeth. In fact, the Spanish "d" is quite close to the English "th" in "brother" and "this."

NOTE: Do <u>NOT</u> use the "th" sound of "thick" or "thin" with the pronunciation guide. The voiceless "th" sound in "thick" is used only in parts of Spain, where it is used instead of an "s" sound for the "z" and "c." Always use the "th" sound in "brother" with the guide.

Whenever you see "d," think "th" as in "brother" and "this."

WHEN YOU SEE	SAY	IT MEANS
adiós	ah-th'YOHSS	good-bye
usted	oo-STETH	You singular (polite)
ustedes	oo-STETH-ehss	You all
nada	NAH-thah	nothing
día*	THEE-ah	day
¿Dónde?*	THOHN-theh	where?

*__NOTE:__ The "th" is easy to say between vowels, where there is a continuous flow of air. The "th" will be muffled when it begins the sound, or comes after a consonant, but the tongue is still <u>between the teeth</u>. You can feel the difference in *nada* vs. *donde* and *cada día* vs. *Buenos días*.

It takes practice to train yourself to say a "the" sound instead of a "da" sound for the Spanish "d," but correct pronunciation is essential to both understand and be understood in Spanish. The reason why it makes such a big difference is that the English "d" said quickly sounds like the Spanish "r."

R & RR

There are two different "r" sounds in Spanish: the **flap** "r" and the **trill** "r."
Even if you can't trill, or roll your "r's" at first, you can still say the flap "r." It
is NOT good Spanish to use an American English "r."

R between vowels

The Spanish name **Miriam**, sounds very much like the English word **medium**.

This is because the Spanish "r" between vowels is a flap, close to the American
English "dd" of "buddy" said QUICKLY. It's not exact, but it's close. If you can
say "medium" and "buddy" FAST, then you can say the Spanish "r" between
vowels.

Whenever you see a single "r" between vowels, think "fast dd."

WHEN YOU SEE	SAY	IT MEANS
Mire.	MEEddeh (MEEdday)	Look. (polite command)
hora	OHddah	hour, time of event
pero	PEHddoh	but
para	PAHddah	(intended) for
número	NOO-mehddoh	number

Before a consonant, "r" still sounds like a FAST "d." To try it, say "today" like
"t'day" three times fast. Then add an –S and say:

tres	t'dehss (t'dayss)	three

Say "g'day" like an Australian three times FAST, change it to "g'dah" and then
try:

Gracias.	g'DAH-s'yahss	Thanks.

Make the sound "tah-DUH" (like when you finish a magic trick), three times
FAST, and then try:

trabajo	t'ddah-BAH-hoh	job, work, project

Now try the single "r" as "dd" in other words:

problema	p'ddoh-BLEH-mah	problem
nombre	NOHM-b'ddeh	name
libro	LEE-b'ddoh	book

NOTE: It's LEE-b'ddoh, <u>not</u> LEEB-ddoh. You're not saying a beginning English "d" of "dog," but the FAST "dd" of "buddy." (You can feel the difference in your mouth when you say **dog** vs. **buddy**.) You have to say the syllable with the "r" sound fast, and you have to say it separately, in order for this trick to work.

Also, don't say an English "r" and "dd" together. It's just one "r," so it's JUST the fast ENGLISH "dd." So, it's <u>not</u> LEE-berdoh, just LEE-b'ddoh.

Finally, remember that the pronunciation guide is to be read as an English nonsense word. So, don't try to say the Spanish "th" sound for the "dd." This is the fast ENGLISH "dd" of "buddy."

Sometimes students think they hear an English "r" when the teacher is speaking Spanish. Perhaps this is because the flap "r" is used in Britain, so American English speakers are used to hearing it. Rest assured that when you pronounce the single, flap "r" as the fast "dd" in "buddy," you will approximate the Spanish sound. Your ears may deceive you until they have become accustomed to the new way of making certain sounds.

Middle RR and End R (RR)

The other Spanish "r" sound is the **trilled**, or rolled "rr."

The trilled "r" occurs any time you see the written "rr," as well as when there is a single "r" at **the beginning** or **the end** of the word or syllable.

If you can purr like a cat, make a motorcycle revving-up sound or say, "Right away, Captain Kirk" with a Scottish accent, you can trill your "r's."

In the pronunciation guide, the "r's" that are trilled are indicated by **rr**.

If you can't trill, try the following trick.

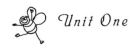

Say the word "ladder," QUICKLY. It will seem strange at first, but the "dder" in "ladder" will get your tongue tapping in the right place for the trilled "rr." It's not perfect, but if you substitute "dder" for each "rr" or final "r," you will be understood.

The hard part isn't actually saying the "dder," but believing that saying it sounds good. If you say it QUICKLY, it will!

Let's say you see the following expression in the pronunciation guide.

| Por favor. | POH*RR* fah-VOH*RR* | Please. |

Now try it with the ladder trick.

| Por favor. | POHdder fah-VOHdder | Please. |

The first part (POHdder) is similar to the word "porter" (a person who carries luggage), said QUICKLY. The last part (VOHdder) is similar to the word "voter" (person who votes), said QUICKLY.

At first, it may feel uncomfortable for you to trill your r's, but it is worth the extra effort. And don't try to say **por favor** as quickly as you can say **please**. It's a longer expression, so give yourself time.

Whenever you see "rr," or an end "r," think "trill."

WHEN YOU SEE	SAY	IT MEANS
carro	CAH-*rr*oh (CAH-dderoh)	car (Mex., parts of L. Am.)
por	POH*RR* (POHdder)	per, for receipt of, for POR-tion of time or $
poner	poh-NAI*RR* (poh-NEHDDER)	to put, place

It looks strange, but it works! Just be sure to say it QUICKLY and to read the "dder" as in the ENGLISH word "ladder."

As with the "dd" used to represent the single "r," remember that the pronunciation guide is to be read as in English. So, don't try to say the Spanish "th" sound for the "dd." This is the fast ENGLISH "dder" of "ladder."

If the ladder trick helps you to approximate the final or middle trilled "r," write in "dder" whenever you see a middle or end *rr* in the pronunciation guide.

The R (RR) at the End of a Syllable

The "r" can also trill at the end of a syllable, before a consonant.

Words with an "r" followed by a consonant are usually problematic for English speakers. Try the "ladder" trick, and stretch the word out so you can pronounce everything.

WHEN YOU SEE	SAY	IT MEANS
Perdón.	pai*rr**-THOHN (pehdder-THOHN)	Excuse me.
verde	BAI*RR**-theh (BEHdder-theh)	green
suerte	SWAI*RR**-teh (SWEHDDER-teh)	luck

*NOTE: Sometimes the guide will substitute "ai" for "eh" before an "r." This is because the vowel in the Spanish syllable **er / AI*RR*** is pronounced similarly to the English word "air," and NOT like the English word "her." Also, a written "v" is often pronounced like an English "b," especially when it starts a word. See the section on "b" vs. "v" for more information.

It is important to not rush the words. The word for "green" (**verde**) sounds very much like the English words "better-they." The first syllable of the word for 'luck' (**suerte**) sounds very much like the English word "sweater." Even though you are saying the "dder" (or "tter") quickly, it will still make the word longer and more complicated to say. Give yourself time.

If you become too frustrated with trying to trill the "r" before a consonant, don't worry. This is one instance where you can use an English "r" and still be understood. Just be sure to say the other letters correctly, such as the vowels and the "th" sound for the "d."

Beginning R as RR

Beginning "r's" are also a trill, but usually a light one. If you can't trill yet, try to say "EHddeh" (almost like "Eddie") three times FAST. Then make like you're going to say "EHddeh," but don't voice the initial "EH." (Written, this might look something like -'ddeh.) If you say it QUICKLY, you will feel your tongue tap the roof of your mouth, close to where the tongue should be to make a trill.

Since the beginning "r" is a very light trill, you can also get by with using the single (flap) "r."

Whenever you see beginning "r," think "trill."

WHEN YOU SEE	SAY	IT MEANS
Repita.	*rr* eh-PEE-<u>t</u>ah (-'ddeh-PEE-<u>t</u>ah)	Repeat (polite).

Final Word on R & RR

The single "r" and double (or trilled) "rr" are **separate sounds** in Spanish and can make a difference in meaning, so you ONLY trill when the pronunciation guide indicates a ***rr***. The single, or flap "r's" are indicated by the English "dd."

Also, you don't have to be able to trill your "r's" in order to start speaking Spanish. Say the single (flap) "r" between vowels and the Spanish "d" and "t" correctly, and you will have an understandable pronunciation, even if you CAN'T trill yet. But keep trying—it's fun!

Now practice saying the different types of "r" together:

WHEN YOU SEE	SAY	IT MEANS
hora	OHddah	hour, time of event
carro	CAH-*rr* oh	car
Por favor.	POH*RR* fah-VOH*RR*	Please.
Gracias.	g'DDAH-s'yahss	Thanks.
para	PAHddah	(intended) for
Repita.	*rr* eh-PEE-<u>t</u>ah	Repeat (polite).

*Write in "dder" when the guide indicates *rr* if you need help saying the middle or final trill.

T

The "t" in Spanish does not have an English equivalent, but is not difficult to pronounce. It is similar to the English "t" in "Tom," but is more muffled, because the tongue is kept next to the back of the teeth. This is important to know because since the Spanish "t" is more muffled, it can sound a little like the English "d" of dark.

First, say the English word "two." Notice how your tongue is in your mouth when you say the "t"—away from the teeth.

Now put your tongue right down against the back of your upper front teeth, as if you were going to spit. (**NOTE:** Your tongue is not **between** your teeth as with the "th" sound for the "d"; it's just making contact **behind** the teeth.)

Now you can say the Spanish word **tú** ("TOO"), which is the intimate way to say "you." Try it again: English word **two**, versus the Spanish word **tú**.

There is no way to write the Spanish "t" in English, so it will be underlined in the pronunciation guide to remind you to put your tongue behind your teeth. If you always remember to do this, you will improve your accent tremendously without too much effort.

More importantly, you will avoid pronouncing a "t" between vowels as a fast "dd" (for example, as in the American English pronunciation of "water"), which, of course, sounds like the Spanish "r."

Whenever you see "t," think "tongue behind the teeth."

WHEN YOU SEE	SAY	IT MEANS
necesito	neh-seh-SEE-toh	I need
minuto	mee-NOO-toh	minute
tengo	TEHNG-goh	I have
está	eh-STAH	is located or feeling
Lo siento.	loh-s'YEHN-toh	I'm sorry.

✿✿✿✿✿✿
Check for Understanding

Along with the vowels, the D, R, and T are the most important Spanish sounds for you to learn. They are confusing at first, because the R is "dd," the D is "th," and the T never sounds like the American "tt" of "butter."

If you are having trouble saying a word, ignore the Spanish spelling and learn the word ONLY from the pronunciation guide. It's much more important that you know how to say the word, than how to spell it. You can learn the spelling later.

Try these three words:

todo	TOH-thoh	all
toro	TOHddoh	bull
Toto (el perro)	TOH-toh	Toto (the dog)

Now try these:

cada	CAH-thah	each
cara	CAHddah	face (also: expensive)
caro	CAHddoh	expensive
carro	CAH-rr oh	car

Now practice saying words with combinations of "d," "r," and "t":

dirección	thee-ddehk-s'YOHN	address
cerca* de	SAIRR-cah theh	near (to)
Repita.	rr eh-PEE-tah	Repeat. (polite)
tarde*	TAHRR –theh	afternoon, late
entrada	ehn-t'DDAH-thah	entrance
computadora	cohm-poo-tah-THOH-ddah	computer
he mirado	eh-mee-DDAH-thoh	I have looked at

*Write in "dder" when the guide indicates *rr* if you need help saying the middle or final trill.

THE "Y" SOUND LETTERS

y

Spanish "y" is usually considered a consonant and may be pronounced like the "y" in "yes." You will see this pronunciation at the beginnings of words and syllables. Examples of words that start with "y" are **yo** / YOH (I, used for emphasis or to answer a Who? question) and **ya** / YAH (already).

Just as in the English words "pretty" and "toy," the Spanish "y" can also sound like the vowel sound "ee" (the Spanish "i"). You will see the letter "y" at the end of a very limited number of words. Some examples are **soy** / SOY (I am-name, definition), **hoy** / OY (today), **hay** / "AYE" (there is, there are), **voy** / VOY (I'm going), and **muy** / MOOY (very).

In rare cases (for example, in the old-fashioned spelling of names), the "y" is used instead of an "i." For example, the name **Isela Ibarra** / ee-SEH-lah ee-BAH-*rr*ah might be written **Ysela Ybarra**.

Also, the Spanish word for "and" is written "**y**" and pronounced "ee." For example: **pluma y papel** / PLOO-mah ee pah-PEHL (pen and paper).

Some speakers will pronounce the "y" (and the "ll," which you will learn next) like a soft "j," so the Spanish word **yo** (I) may sound like "joh." Other speakers will make a softer sound for the "y," like the "s" in "leisure." This is something to be aware of and listen for, but you don't need to imitate it. A "y" sound will always be understood.

Whenever you see "y," think "y" like in English.

WHEN YOU SEE	SAY	IT MEANS
yo	yoh	I (used for emphasis or to answer "Who?")
ya	yah	already
soy...	soy	I'm... (name)
hay	"aye" (or "eye")	there is, there are
y	ee	and

LL (not L)

The single Spanish "l" of **clase** / CLAH-seh and **material** / mah-<u>t</u>ehddee-AHL is pronounced with the tongue curved up next to the teeth, so it's a little higher and crisper than the relaxed English "l" of **class** and **material**, but if you say the English "l" you will be understood.

However, the double "ll" is most easily pronounced similar to the Spanish "y." There are a variety of regional pronunciations, but a "y" sound will always be understood.

Whenever you see single "L" think "L."
BUT

Whenever you see double "ll," think "y."

WHEN YOU SEE	SAY	IT MEANS
calle	CAH-yeh	street
amarillo	ah-mahDDEE-yoh	yellow
se llama	seh-YAH-mah	is called (calls itself)

Ñ (not N)

The plain "n" is like the English "n." However, the "ñ" with the tilde (wavy line) is like the "ny" in "canyon." The "ñ" with the tilde and the "n" without the tilde are completely different sounds, and can make a difference in meaning.

Whenever you see "n," think "n."
BUT

Whenever you see "ñ," think "ny."

WHEN YOU SEE	SAY	IT MEANS
niños	NEEN-yohs	children
año	AHN-yoh	year
baño	BAHN-yoh	bathroom
español	eh-spahn-YOHL	Spanish

"H" AND THE "H" SOUND LETTERS

H

The Spanish "h" is ALWAYS silent, as the "h" in the English word "hour."

Whenever you see "h," think "silent, so ignore it."

WHEN YOU SEE	SAY	IT MEANS
hablo	AH-bloh	I speak
hoy	OY	today
hay	AYE (like "I" or "eye")	there is, there are
ha	AH	You have (done)

J, G before e and i, and X

The Spanish "j" is like the "h" sound in the English word "happy." Spanish "j" can be soft or more raspy, depending on the dialect of the speaker.

The Spanish "g" before "e" and "i" is also like the English "h" of "happy" (soft or more raspy, depending on the dialect of the speaker). Before "a," "e," "o," and consonants, however, the "g" is close to the English "g" of "go."

"X" is usually pronounced as in English, but in a few names of people and places it can represent an "h" sound. A notable example is **México** / MEH-hee-coh, which can also be spelled **Méjico**. Other examples are **Xavier** (Javier), and **Don Quixote (Don Quijote)**.

Whenever you see "j" (and "g" before e or i), think English "h."

WHEN YOU SEE	SAY	IT MEANS
trabajo	t'ddah-BAH-hoh	job, workplace
joven	HOH-vehn	young person
junta	HOON-tah	meeting
la gente	lah HEHN-teh	people (singular)
página	PAH-hee-nah	page

GO GO (GOO GOO, GAH GAH):
THE OTHER G SOUND

G (a,o,u) and Gu (e,i)

The Spanish "g" in **ge** / HEH and **gi** / HEE is a "huh" sound. Otherwise, the "g" is similar to the "guh" sound in the English word "go." In order to indicate a "guh" sound before "e" and "i," a silent "u" is added. So, you say **ga** / GAH, **gue** / GEH, **gui** / GHEE, **go** / GOH, and **gu** / GOO, with the "g" as in "go."

Whenever you see "g" (a, o, u) and "gu" (e, i), think "g" as in "go."

WHEN YOU SEE	SAY	IT MEANS
amigos	ah-MEE-gohs	friends
agua	AH-gwah	water
guitarra*	ghee-TAH-*rr*ah	guitar

*If you can't say the trill yet, substitute "dder" for each middle or final *rr* in the guide.

NOTE: Sometimes speakers say the "g" toward the back of the throat and so softly that the "g" disappears. So, **Guadalupe** can sound like wah-thah-LOO-peh, **saguaro** like sah-WAH-ddoh, and **agua** like AH-wah.

If the "u" has two dots on it (ü), you do pronounce the "u" as "w." This is not common.

bilingüe	bee-LEENG-gweh	bilingual

VERY GOOD OR BERRY GOOD?

B and V

For practical purposes, Spanish "b" and the "v" are the same letter. A word that begins with a "v" will often be pronounced with a "b" sound. Sometimes a "b" in the middle of a word will sound more like a "v." The pronunciation guide will indicate the best way for you to pronounce "b" and "v."

Whenever you see "b" or "v," think "interchangeable."

WHEN YOU SEE	SAY	IT MEANS
¡Vamos!	BAH-mohss VAH-mohss	Let's go!

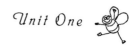

THE "K" SOUND LETTERS

QU, C, and K

The "u" in the Spanish "qu" is silent, so "qu" is a "k" sound. (Imagine that the English word **queen** were pronounced "keen.")

As in the English words **cat**, **cot**, and **cut**, the Spanish "c" before "a," "o," and "u" is a "k" sound. The "kw" sound is spelled "cu." (Imagine that the English word "queen" (kween) would have to be written out as **cueen**.)

The letter "k" is used only in words of foreign origin, like **kilómetro** (kilometer).

Whenever you see "qu" (and "c" before a, o, & u), think "k."

WHEN YOU SEE	SAY	IT MEANS
¿qué?, que	KEH (close to KAY)	what?, that
aquí	ah-KEE	here
quiero	k'YEHddoh	I want
¿cuándo?, cuando	KWAHN-thoh	when?, when

THE "S" SOUND LETTERS

S, Z (and C before e and i)

The Spanish "s" is like the English "s." Everywhere except Spain, the "z" (and the "c" before "e" and "i") are also an "s" sound. (In parts of Spain, the "z" and the "c" before "e" and "i" are the voiceless "th" sound of "thick" and "thin.")

Whenever you see "s," "z," (and "c" before e or i), think "s."

WHEN YOU SEE	SAY	IT MEANS
Lo siento.	loh S'YEHN-toh	I'm sorry.
Gracias.	g'DDAH-s'yahss	Thanks.
lápiz	LAH-peess	pencil
azul	ah-SOOL	blue
dirección*	thee-ddehk-s'YOHN	address

*The first "c" is a hard "k" sound; the second is a soft "s" sound.

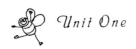
STRESS AND ACCENT MARKS

Spanish has rules for where to stress or emphasize words with your voice. The rules are:

Words ending in a vowel (or vowel plus –S or –N) are stressed on the **next-to last** syllable. Words ending in a consonant (except –S or –N) are stressed on the **last** syllable. Words that break these rules are spelled with an accent mark. Stress goes on the vowel with the accent mark.

The pronunciation guide always indicates with CAPITAL LETTERS where a word should be stressed, so for now, just remember that...

You ALWAYS stress the written accent mark if there is one.

Ends in a vowel, –S, or –N: Stress the second to last syllable

señora	sehn-YOHddah	Ma'am, Mrs., lady
señorita	sehn-yohDDEE-tah	Miss, young lady
libros	LEE-b'ddohss	books
necesitan	neh-seh-SEE-tahn	You all, they need

Ends in a consonant (NOT –S or –N): Stress the last syllable

señor	sehn-YOHRR	Sir, Mr., gentleman
usted	oo-STETH	You (singular, polite)
español	eh-spahn-YOHL	Spanish

Breaks the rule: Stress the vowel with the written accent mark

lápiz	LAH-pees	pencil
número	NOO-meddoh	number
está	eh-STAH	is located, is feeling
allá	ah-YAH	over there
dirección	thee-ddehk-s'YOHN	address
teléfono	teh-LEH-foh-noh	telephone

NOTE: Put <u>plenty</u> of emphasis on the syllable that should be stressed. Often English speakers do not put enough emphasis on the ONE syllable that should be stressed more than all the others. This is especially true in words such as dire<u>cción</u> or tel<u>é</u>fono, which look like English words, but are stressed differently.

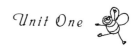

FINAL NOTES

Now you know the basics of how to pronounce Spanish!

Dictionaries and other pronunciation guides often do not give the "closest" English approximation for sounds such as Spanish "d" and "r," and instead take the easy way out. This does not mean that it is desirable to pronounce Spanish letters as in English. You may have to rewrite those pronunciation guides or ignore them, based on what you will learn in this course. Of course, once you have learned Spanish letter-sound relationships, you won't need a pronunciation guide anymore.

Be sure to learn new vocabulary with correct, understandable pronunciation. This will influence not only how you speak Spanish, but also how well you will be able to understand it.

Lesson One Expressions

Hola	OH-lah	Hi (Said to a close friend or acquaintance.)
Buenos días	BWEH-nohss THEE-ahss	Good morning (Used to greet a stranger, professional, non-family , etc.)
Por favor*	POH*RR* fah-VOH*RR*	Please
Gracias	g'DDAH-s'yahss	Thanks
De nada	theh NAH-thah	You're welcome (Literally "of nothing")
Un momento.	oon moh-MEHN-toh	One moment.

*Write in "dder" when the guide indicates *rr* if you need help saying the middle or final trill.

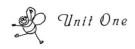

Practice With Names

GIRLS		BOYS	
María	mahDDEE-ah	Mario	MAHddeeoh
Leticia	leh-<u>TEE</u>-s'yah	Alejandro	ah-leh-HAHN-th'ddoh
Ana	AH-nah	Jesús	heh-SOOS
Gisela	hee-SEH-lah	Eduardo	eh-th'WAH*rr*-thoh
Teresa	<u>teh</u>DDEH-sah	Jorge	HOH*rr*-heh
Verónica	behDDOH-nee-cah	Manuel	mahn-WEHL
Claudia	CLOU-thee-ah *with ou of cloud*	Luis	looWEESS *said as one syllable*
Cristina	k'ddee-S<u>TEE</u>-nah	David	thah-VEETH
Guadalupe	<u>g</u>wah-thah-LOO-peh	José	hoh-SSEH
Marta	MAH*rr*-<u>t</u>ah	Fernando	fai*rr*-NAHN-thoh
Eva	EH-vah	Miguel	mee-GEHL
Julia	HOOL-yah	Roberto	*rr* oh-BAI*rr*-<u>t</u>oh

SURNAMES			
Padilla	pah-THEE-yah	Gómez	GOH-mehss
Rivera	*rr* ee-BEHddah	Villanova	bee-yah-NOH-vah
Muñoz	moon-YOHSS	Vásquez	BAHSS-kehss
Rodríguez	*rr* oh-th'DEE-guess	Hernández	ai*rr*-NAHN-thess
Mendoza	mehn-THOH-ssah	Flores	FLOH-ddehss

TITLES		
señor	sehn-YOH*RR*	Sir, Mr.
señora	sehn-YOHddah	Ma'am, Mrs.
señorita	sehn-yohDDEE-<u>t</u>ah	Miss

*Write in "dder" when the guide indicates *rr* if you need help saying the middle or final trill.

Read these combinations, and then make others of your own:

María Padilla, Luis Vásquez, Ana Muñoz, José Rodríguez,
Leticia Rivera, Claudia Gómez, Jorge Flores, Manuel Mendoza,
señora Padilla, señor Vásquez, señora Muñoz, señor Rodríguez

Speaking Practice

Practice saying the words in Lesson One, using the pronunciation gui
checkmark next to the challenging words. Repeat these words seve
Think of it like learning to play a musical instrument or a sport. It w
practice to train your mind and body to speak Spanish.

Speaking Activities

Check your pronunciation with a partner. Partner #1 reads the Spanish words aloud, looking ONLY at the Spanish column. Partner #2 listens to the Spanish words and looks ONLY at the pronunciation guide column.

If Partner #1's pronunciation is not correct, Partner #2 must say **¿Cómo? /
COH-moh?**, which is a polite way to say "What?" when you don't hear or understand something.

More Practice

1) Practice reading words aloud from Lesson One, using the pronunciation guide. Refer to the "Saying & Understanding" chart on page 1-4 and the Lesson One text. Listen to the audio program if you have it.
2) Say the names in "Practice with Names," using the pronunciation guide. Then, use the Lesson One expressions to make up greetings, such as:

> --¡Hola, María! (Hi, Maria!)
> --Ana Gómez, por favor. (Ana Gomez, please.)
> --Buenos días, señor Padilla. (Good morning, Mr. Padilla.)
> --Gracias, Roberto. (Thanks, Roberto.)
> --De nada, señora Flores. (You're welcome, Mrs. Flores.)

2) Learn to say **gracias, por favor**, and **de nada** with correct pronunciation.
3) Read Spanish words aloud from another source, such as a book, dictionary, or phrase list. If there is a pronunciation guide, check it for accuracy based on what you now know.
4) Practice saying words commonly known to American English speakers such as "adiós" and "enchilada" with correct Spanish pronunciation.
5) Visit **www.spanishthatworks.org** for additional suggestions, practice materials, and links to other resources.

Lesson One Mini-Dialogues: Greetings

A) Greeting family, close friend or acquaintance, co-worker your age

1) Hola, _____.	1) Hi, _____.
2) Hola, _____.	2) Hi, _____.

NAMES: Ana / AH-nah, **Mario** / MAH-ddee-oh, **Eva** / EH-vah, **Luis** / looWEES, **Verónica** / behDDOH-nee-cah, **David** / thah-VEETH, **Julia** / HOO-lee-ah, **Señora Villa** / sehn-YOHddah BEE-yah, **Señor Gómez**, sehn-YOHRR GOH-mehss **Señorita Mendoza** / sehn-yohDDEE-tah mehn-THOH-sah, **OTHER**

B) Greeting a stranger, professional acquaintance

1) Buenos días, _____.	1) Good morning, _____.
2) Buenos días, _____.	2) Good morning, _____.

C) Requesting someone by name

1) _____, por favor.	1) _____, please.
2) Un momento. *Goes to call person.*	2) One moment. *Goes to call person.*
1) Gracias.	1) You're welcome.

NAMES: **María Hernández** / mahDDEE-ah ai*rr*-NAHN-thehss, **David Cendón** / thah-VEETH sehn-THOHN, **Leticia Paz** / leh-TEE-s'yah PAHSS **José Flores** / hoh-SEH FLOHddehss, **Luz Rivera** / LOOS *rr*ee-BEHddah, **OTHER**

D) Saying thanks

1) *Presents item.*	1) *Presents item.*
2) Gracias. *Takes item.*	2) Thanks. *Takes item.*
1) De nada.	1) You're welcome.

KEY: _____ Insert names from list
Action Instructions for role-play

EXTRA NOTE:

With an older person for whom one has
both respect and affection, the titles
don / THOHN (for a man) and
doña / THOHN-yah (for a woman) are sometimes
used with the first name, instead of the more
impersonal terms **señor** and **señora**.

So, you might call your neighbors
don José and **doña Luisa**,
instead of **señor** and **señora Rivera**, in order to
show respect with a more personal touch.

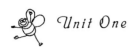

LESSON TWO: Things

A) BASIC THINGS

nombre (m.)	NOHM-b'ddeh	name
número	NOO-meh-ddoh	number
dirección (f.)	thee-ddehk-s'YOHN	address
libro	LEE-b'ddoh	book
trabajo	t'ddah-BAH-hoh	work, job, project
tarjeta	tahrr-HEH-tah	card
lápiz (m.)	LAH-pees	pencil
pluma	PLOO-mah	pen
papel (m.)	pah-PEHL	paper
teléfono	teh-LEH-foh-noh	telephone
computadora	cohm-poo-tah-THOHddah	computer
clase (f.)	CLAH-seh	class

*Write in "dder" when the guide indicates *rr* if you need help saying the middle or final trill.

Variety in vocabulary

Just as English often has several words to describe the same thing (such as **exam, test, assessment**, and **quiz**), there is sometimes more than one correct word for something in Spanish.

For example, a computer may be referred to as a **computadora, computador,** or **ordenador**, depending on the origin of the speaker. Words for "pen" include **pluma, lapicero,** and **bolígrafo.**

You want to learn standard vocabulary whenever possible, so that others will understand you. The words and expressions in *Spanish that Works* were chosen for practicality and are considered to be standard Latin American Spanish. Some speakers may prefer to use other vocabulary, but they should understand the terms you are studying. For instance, a Mexican speaker might refer to an identification card as a **credencial (f.)**, while a Spaniard would use the word **carnet (m.)**, but both should understand the word **tarjeta.**

The (m.) and (f.) refer to noun gender, which is explained in Lesson Four. You can find more information about variety in Spanish in the supplemental section.

...LTY THINGS (optional)

...or make up, a list of additional <u>items</u> (things you may have, need, or ...an..., ...a. are essential for communication at your job or in your life. You may ask your teacher or visit **www.spanishthatworks.org** for ideas. If you use a dictionary, make sure each word is a noun (person, place or thing). A noun may be indicated by **n.** (nombre, noun) or **s.** (sustantivo). You should also note the noun's gender (**m.** or **f.**). Look up the word on the Spanish side of the dictionary to find the gender (if not listed) and to double-check the translation.

Make a pronunciation guide for your specialty words, using the chart on page 1-4. Then fill out this blank chart with the twelve most important words. It's fine if some of the specialty items overlap with the basic things words.

SPANISH	PRONUNCIATION	ENGLISH

Check for Understanding

Practice saying your "Things" words, both basic and specialty, until you are familiar with them. Then read the section on "How to Practice Vocabulary."

C) HOW TO PRACTICE VOCABULARY

You can study from the word lists in the course text and supplemental section, and from any specialty lists you may have. You should also make flashcards on 3 X 5 index cards or visit **www.spanishthatworks.org** for information about cut-out flashcard pages. If you make your own flashcards, include a pronunciation guide. Follow these steps when learning new words from either flashcards or word lists.

1) Rehearsing: Saying & Learning

Work with a partner, if possible, and use flashcards if you have them. Read the Spanish words aloud, paying attention to correct pronunciation. Use the pronunciation guide to approximate the Spanish sounds.

If you are having difficulty saying the Spanish letters, practice the words looking ONLY at the pronunciation guide. This is a conversation course, so the sound is more important than the spelling.

After you say the word, look at its meaning (English word). Do this until you are familiar with the meanings of the words. Think up a visualization, sound-alike word, or other device to jog your memory for the words.

For example, to recall the Spanish word for "pen" (**pluma**), you might visualize using a feather plume, as in an old-fashioned quill pen. **Pen—plume—pluma / PLOO-mah.**

The best memory devices will reflect the Spanish pronunciation, since this is a conversation course and it's more important to know how to say the words than to know how to spell them. However, sometimes you might have to use a word association that is closer to spelling than sound. For example, to remember the Spanish word for "card" (**tarjeta**), you might imagine yourself going to a Target store to buy a birthday card and paying for it with your credit card. **Card—Target—tarjeta / tahrr-HEH-tah.**

If possible, have someone with native or near-native pronunciation of Latin American Spanish help you say the words correctly.

Quiz yourself with your flashcards or word list by reading the Spanish side with the English word covered. Check yourself after each word by looking at the English side. If you don't know one, rehearse the word and then put it aside (flashcard) or put a checkmark by it (list). When you finish all the words in the set, go back and quiz yourself again on the words you didn't know. Use memory devices to help you remember the words better next time.

Working with a partner

If you are working with a partner, you will each take turns being the **teacher** partner and the **student** partner for each step. The partner who knows the material better or feels more confident should be the student first.

The teacher partner says and shows the Spanish word to the student partner. The student partner repeats the Spanish and says what the word means in English. If the student partner doesn't know one, the teacher partner gives the correct answer and puts the flashcard aside or makes a checkmark on the list. After each set, the teacher helps the student rehearse the unfamiliar words and come up with memory devices for the difficult ones.

Teacher and student switch roles and repeat step number two before going on to step number three.

3) Quiz: Saying the Spanish

On your own

Quiz yourself with the flashcards or the word list by reading the English side with the Spanish word covered. Check yourself after each word by showing the English side. If you don't know one, rehearse the word and then put it aside or put a checkmark by it on the list. When you finish all the words in the set, go back and quiz yourself again on the words you didn't know. Practice the ones you didn't remember until you know them, using memory devices when necessary.

Working with a partner

The teacher partner shows and says the English word, and the student partner says what the word means in Spanish. If the student doesn't know one, the teacher says and shows the correct answer and then puts the flashcard aside or makes a checkmark on the list. After each set, the teacher partner helps the student rehearse the unfamiliar words and come up with memory devices for the challenging ones. The partners switch roles and repeat the process before going on to another set of words.

Using Spanish in partner practice

To practice speaking in Spanish as you and your partner quiz each other, use the following expressions:

Student partner: If you don't know one, say **No sé** / noh-SEH, or "I don't know." Remember it this way: if you **don't know**, you can't **say**. "No sé" (sounds like "no say") means "I don't know."

Teacher partner: Don't give the student the answer until he or she says **No sé**. If the student is not using good pronunciation on a word, say **¿Cómo?** / COH-moh?, which is a polite way to say "What?" when you don't understand someone.

When the student misses a words, say **No** / noh which means "No." When the student gets a word right, say **Sí** / SEE, which means "Yes." At the end of each set, you can use the expression **¡Muy bien!** / mooy b'YEHN which means "Very well (done)!"

Building Fluency

Go through the words or dialogues at least once a day to build fluency. Practice until the words are so easy that you can remember them without having to think at all. Then practice some more, to improve your pronunciation and speed of recall.

When learning new words, follow all three steps in "How to Practice Vocabulary." When doing review work, you may skip step number one.

Lesson Two Expressions

Buenos días	BWEH-nohss THEE-ahss	Good morning, Good day (Hello)
Buenas tardes*	BWEH-nahss TAH*rr*-thehss	Good afternoon, Good evening (Hello)
señor*	sehn-YOH*RR*	Sir, Mr.
señora	sehn-YOHddah	Ma'am, Mrs.
señorita	sehn-yohDDEE-tah	Young woman, Miss
joven	HOH-vehn	Young man
Un momento.	oon moh-MEHN-toh	One moment.
Por favor.*	POH*RR* fah-VOH*RR*	Please.
Gracias.	g'DDAH-s'yahss	Thanks.
De nada.	theh NAH-thah	You're welcome. (Literally "of nothing")
su	soo	Your, his, her, their
mi	mee	my

* Write in "dder" whenever you see *rr* if you need help saying the trill.

NOTES: To learn **mi** and **su**, remember that **my** things belong to "me" = **mi** (my), and you can "sue" = **su** someone to get **his, her, their,** or **Your** things. (Spanish objects have gender, so **su** sometimes translates into English as **its**.)

The words "You" and "Your" are often capitalized in *Spanish that Works* to show that you are using the polite form of address. With a child or close personal friend, native speakers may use the word **tu** (instead of **su**), which is the "buddy-buddy" way to say "your." In this course, you will practice only the polite, professional "Your" (**su**). Refer to the supplemental section for more information on the different ways to say "you" and "your."

Note that **su** does not mean "You." It means **Your (his, her, their)**. The polite word for "You" is **usted** / oo-STETH, and is covered in Lesson Four.

Finally, **Buenos días** and **Buenas tardes** are often used where an English speaker would say "hello." The word **hola** / OH-lah is closer to the word "hi," and is used with friends and family. You may also wish to learn the expression **Buenas noches** / BWEH-nahss NOH-chess (Good night), which is used late in the evening or at night after dark. You would say **Buenas noches** to greet someone at night, to leave a place for the evening, or to go to sleep at night.

Speaking Practice

1) Practice saying the Lesson Two expressions until you are familiar with ...
Follow the instructions in "How to Practice Vocabulary" on pages 1-29 to 1-30.
Work with a partner, if possible.

2) Make a separate list or flashcards for the "Things" words (basic or specialty) and use them to practice the Lesson Two mini-dialogues on page 1-36. Be sure to **follow the steps** outlined in "How to Use the Mini-Dialogues" in the next section (pages 1-34 and 1-35). (NOTE: Although the word **su** can also mean **his, her, its,** and **their**, it is understood by context that **su** means **Your** in the Lesson Two mini-dialogues.)

Speaking Activity

Pick a dialogue and act it out. Work with a partner, and use props, if possible.

More Practice

1) Say the "Things" words and the Lesson Two expressions aloud using the pronunciation guide. Work with a partner if possible.

2) Learn the Lesson Two expressions and the "Basic Things" words by heart. It's good to use flashcards. Be able to both understand and speak the Spanish.

3) Practice any specialty vocabulary.

4) Visit **www.spanishthatworks.org** for additional suggestions, practice materials, and links to other resources.

How to Use the Mini-Dialogues

The purpose of this course is for you to build fluency with key vocabulary words and expressions. The main way that you will get speaking practice in this course is through the mini-dialogues. The mini-dialogues (also referred to as "dialogues") allow you to practice the vocabulary and expressions within contexts that are likely to occur in real life. The dialogues are simplified in order to facilitate memorization and build fluency.

Please **follow these steps** when using the mini-dialogues. For additional information or for specialty dialogues, visit **www.spanishthatworks.org**.

1) After each lesson, you will use the mini-dialogues to practice vocabulary and expressions. Read each dialogue aloud. You will make choices among the words within parentheses (the choices are divided by slash marks). You will insert vocabulary words into the underlined spaces, according to the type of word (item, place, action, etc.). The words in italics are instructions for role-play.

2) If you are working alone, read both parts of the dialogue. If you are working with a partner, **ALTERNATE** who goes first **each time** you say the dialogue, so that you each practice both parts equally.

3) Go through **each** dialogue **once** for **EACH** vocabulary item. Sometimes you will be given a list and sometimes you will be asked to use your flashcards. **Go in the order** of the list or your flashcards as you practice each dialogue. The purpose is to build fluency with all the words, not to pick out the things you like.

For example, read dialogue A in the Lesson Two mini-dialogues once using the names **Ana & Mario**, and then again, using the names **Jesús & Eva**, and then again using **Julia & Luis**, until you have gone through the entire list, including the OTHER option, which allows you to insert additional words from the text or your own life experience.

For dialogue B you will use your "Things" flashcards. Draw a new flashcard each time you say the dialogue and insert that word into the item blank. The first time you say dialogue B, you might draw the word **nombre** for the item, the second time you do dialogue B you might use the word **número**, and the third time you do dialogue B, you might say **dirección**.

REPEAT the dialogue in this fashion until you have gone through the **entire list** or <u>**ALL**</u> of your flashcards. Do this for each and every dialogue. This means that you will go through most of the dialogues at least twelve times before moving on to the next.

NOTE: You can practice the "Basic Things" words separately, or you can mix them in with other "Things" words from your specialty vocabulary. Practice with no more than twelve to fifteen words at a time, and start with the words that are most important for you to know.

4) When you have finished with **all** of the words for **one dialogue**, you can go on to the next one. Repeat the process in steps one, two, and three. **Don't jump around** between dialogues. Practice each dialogue over and over until you are finished with the list or your set of flashcards.

5) There is no pronunciation guide in the dialogues. If necessary, **make notes** on the dialogue so you say the words correctly. Use the pronunciation guide in your text to help you.

6) Some words will not make perfect sense in the context of the dialogue, but you can say them anyway, **just for fun.**

7) The **more you practice** the dialogues, the **more fluent** your Spanish will become. Use the dialogues to review material, and memorize the dialogues that you feel will be most useful to you. If you are in a class and you finish going through all the dialogues before it is time to stop, go back and practice the dialogues again, giving extra attention to pronunciation and fluency.

8) If you are in a class, you and a partner may act out a dialogue for your classmates. **Use props** if you can, to make the dialogue seem more realistic.

9) If you are assigned to write an original dialogue, **don't think of a dialogue in English** and attempt to translate it. Use the structures and vocabulary already in the dialogues, and just rearrange the material in a **creative way**. That way, you will be thinking in Spanish, and you will come up with a dialogue that you and all your classmates can understand.

One

Lesson Two Mini-Dialogues:
Things

A) Greeting someone by name

1) (Buenos días / Buenas tardes), _____.	1) (Good morning / afternoon), _____.
2) (Buenos días / Buenas tardes), _____.	2) (Good morning / afternoon), _____.

NAMES: Ana /Mario, Jesús / Eva, Julia / Luis, Verónica / Roberto, Señora Padilla / Señor Gómez, Señorita Mendoza / Señor Vásquez, OTHER

B) Requesting something from someone

1) Su <u>item</u>, por favor.	1) Your <u>item</u>, please.
2) Un momento. *Presents item.*	2) One moment. *Presents item.*
1) Gracias. *Takes item.*	1) Thanks. *Takes item.*

C) Giving something to someone

1) (Buenos días / Buenas tardes). Mi <u>item</u>. *Presents item.*	1) Hello. My <u>item</u>. *Presents item.*
2) Gracias. *Takes item.*	2) Thanks. *Takes item.*
1) De nada.	1) You're welcome.

D) When someone forgets something

1) ¡(Señor / Señora / Señorita /Joven)! ¡Su <u>item</u>!	1) (Sir / Ma'am / Miss / Young man)! Your <u>item</u>!
2) ¡Ah! ¡Gracias! *Takes item.*	2) Oh! Thanks! *Takes item.*
1) De nada.	1) You're welcome.

KEY: (x / y)   *Make a choice among words*

_____   *Insert words from flashcards or list*

Action   *Instructions for role-play*

EXTRA NOTE:

In English, if someone asks if you want something,
and the answer is "yes," you say "Yes, please."

However, in Spanish, you use **por favor** (please)
when requesting something, and **gracias** (thanks)
when accepting something.

So, if someone offers you something, you
say **Sí, gracias** (Yes, thanks) to accept it.

If you want someone to give you something, you
say **"Por favor"** (please) to request the item.

UNIT TWO:

"Do you have a pen or a pencil?"

Lesson 3: More About Things

- ❖ More than One Thing: Plural -S / -ES
- ❖ Describing With Nouns
- ❖ Functional Words (In, on, for, from, with, and, or...)
- ❖ More Nouns (Spanish, English, children...)
- ❖ Describing with Nouns ~ Examples
- ❖ Talking about Specialty Things
- ❖ Expressions (My, Your – plural)
- ❖ Mini-Dialogues

Lesson 4: Do you have...?

- ❖ How Verbs Change to Show Who: I/ You, have
- ❖ How to Say No, Not, and Don't
- ❖ How to Say "A" Thing
- ❖ Expressions (Yes, no, but, I'm sorry, of course...)
- ❖ Mini-Dialogues

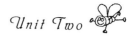

LESSON THREE: More About Things

Basic Structures

A) MORE THAN ONE THING: Plural -S and -ES

A noun is a person, place, thing, or idea. To make Spanish nouns plural, add -S to a word ending in a vowel and -ES to a word ending in a consonant.

> **libro, libros** (book, books)
> **papel, papeles** (paper, papers)

In Spanish, adjectives must match, or agree with the noun. So, if you add an -S to the noun, you also add an -S to **mi** (my) and **su** (Your). (NOTE: Although su(s) can also mean "his," "her," "its," and "their;" in this course, you will usually use su(s) to mean "Your.")

> **mi libro, mis libros** (my book, my books)
> **su papel, sus papeles** (Your paper, Your papers)

Remember, the -S on **sus** (Your) means that You have **more than one possession**. The -S on **sus** has nothing to do with the number of owners.

> **If you add an -S to the noun, you add an -S to "mi" and "su."**

Check for Understanding

1) Go through your "Things" words (basic or specialty) from Lesson Two, making each noun plural by adding -S or -ES. The plurals of the "Basic Things" words are listed in the "Check for Understanding" answer key (starts on page S-53 of the supplemental section).

2) Use the plural "Things" words in place of <u>items</u> in the following mini-dialogue:

> Q. ¿Sus <u>items</u>? (Your <u>items</u>?)
> A. Sí, mis <u>items</u>. (Yes, my <u>items</u>.)

NOTE: The dialogues use English words (<u>item, place, action</u>, etc.) to let you know what kinds of words you should use to fill in the underlined space.

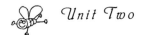

B) DESCRIBING WITH NOUNS

You can use these functional words and a describing noun to talk about various kinds of things.

Functional Words

en	ehn	in, on, at a place
para	PAHddah	(intended) for
por	poh*rr*	for (receipt of), per, for portion of time or $
de	theh	of, from, about a topic, belonging to
con	cohn	with
sin	seen	without
y	ee	and
o	oh	or

NOTE: "Para" and "por" can both translate as "for" in English. "Por" is covered in Lesson Thirteen and "para vs. por" is explained in the supplemental section. For now, just learn "para" and "por" with the translations given.

More Nouns

español (m.)	eh-spahn-YOHL	Spanish
inglés (m.)	een-GLEHSS	English
niños	NEEN-yohss	children
casa	CAH-sah	home, house
mañana	mahn-YAH-nah	tomorrow (also: morning)
usted	oo-STETH	You (polite form)
la familia	lah fah-MEEL-yah	the family

To use the "Describing with Nouns" words, say the <u>item</u> or other noun, a functional word (**en, para, de, con, y, o**) and then another (describing) noun. For example: <u>libro</u> **en español** (<u>book</u> in Spanish) <u>libro</u> **para niños** (<u>book</u> for children), or <u>libro</u> **de inglés** (<u>book</u> of English, or English <u>book</u>). Please note that in English, you can describe a noun by putting another noun in front of it: **Spanish** + <u>book</u>, **telephone** + <u>number</u>, **English** + <u>class</u>. However, in Spanish, putting two nouns together in this way DOES NOT MAKE SENSE.

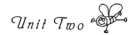

In Spanish, the main noun (in this case, the <u>thing</u> you are describing) always goes FIRST. The describing noun goes SECOND. Often the word **de** (of, from, belonging to) is used to join the two nouns.

So, you say <u>libro</u> **de español** (<u>book</u> of Spanish), <u>**número**</u> **de teléfono** (<u>number</u> of telephone), and <u>**clase**</u> **de inglés** (<u>class</u> of English).

You can use many nouns to describe other nouns. These nouns may be mixed and matched to convey different meanings. For example:

número de trabajo	work number
trabajo en casa	work at home
casa para niños	house for children
número de niños	number of children
número de teléfono de casa	home telephone number

You can string more than one expression together, as in <u>**libros**</u> **en inglés y español para niños** (<u>books</u> in English and Spanish for children) and <u>**número**</u> **de teléfono de casa o de trabajo** (home or work telephone <u>number</u>).

Please note that the second (describing) noun does <u>not</u> automatically change to "match" the first. A noun is a separate and independent concept, so changing the form of the noun changes its meaning. For example, **libros de <u>español</u>** (books of <u>Spanish</u>) is different from **libros de <u>españoles</u>** (books of <u>Spaniards</u>). You must always use the form of the noun that expresses what you mean.

Check for Understanding

Describing Nouns. Translate to Spanish. Use your "Things" words and "Describing With Nouns ~ Examples." Answers in the supplemental section.

1) work in class

2) telephone for You (polite, singular)

3) number of pens

4) pencil or pen

5) work with computers

6) pencil and paper

7) book without paper

8) Spanish book (book of Spanish)

Describing with Nouns ~ Examples

en inglés	ehn een-GLEHSS	in English
en español	ehn eh-spahn-YOHL	in Spanish
en clase	ehn CLAH-seh	in class
en casa	ehn CAH-sah	at home
en el trabajo	ehn ehl t'ddah-BAH-hoh	at work
en _____	ehn _____	in, at, on _____

para niños	PAHddah NEEN-yohss	(intended) for children
para mañana	PAHddah mahn-YAH-nah	(intended) for tomorrow
para usted	PAHddah oo-STETH	(intended) for You
para _____	PAHddah _____	(intended) for _____

por cincuenta (50) centavos	pohrr seen-KWEHN-tah sehn-TAH-vohss	for (receipt of) 50 cents
por tres diás	pohrr t'ddehss THEE-ahss	for (portion of time) three days

_____ de casa	theh CAH-sah	home _____
_____ de trabajo	theh t'ddah-BAH-hoh	work _____
de usted	theh oo-STETH	belonging to You
_____ de Ana	theh AH-nah	Ana's _____
de _____	theh _____	of, about, from _____

con lápiz	cohn LAH-pees	with pencil
con pluma	cohn PLOO-mah	with pen
con la familia	cohn lah fah-MEEL-yah	with the family
sin papel	seen pah-PEHL	without paper

nombre y dirección	NOHM-b'ddeh ee theeddehk-s'YOHN	name and address
papel y lápiz	pah-PEHL ee LAH-pees	paper and pencil
pluma o lápiz	PLOO-mah oh LAH-pees	pen or pencil

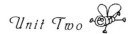

Nouns vs. Adjectives

As you learn how to describe nouns using other nouns, it is important to keep in mind the difference between a **noun** and an **adjective**.

A **noun** is a person, place, thing or idea—something that exists. When it changes form, it changes meaning. For example, **niño** is boy, **niña** is girl, and **niños** are children.

An **adjective**, such as **bueno** (good), is a word that describes a noun directly, without a functional word (en, para, de, etc.) in between. Spanish adjectives <u>do</u> change form to match a noun. So a "good boy" is a **niño bueno**, a "good girl" is a **niña buena**, and "good children" are **niños buenos**. (NOTE: Spanish descriptive adjectives such as **good, beautiful**, and **big** usually go <u>after</u> the noun.)

Unlike nouns, when adjectives change form, the translated meaning does <u>not</u> change. For example, the adjective **bueno** changes from **niño bueno** (good boy) to **niña buena** (good girl), but it still means "good" in both cases.

You will not be using many adjectives in this course, so for now, noun-adjective agreement is just something for you to be aware of. This said, when you <u>do</u> come across an expression which includes an adjective (such as **Buenos días** or **Buenas tardes**), be sure to learn the adjective with its correct ending. For more information on adjectives, please refer to the supplemental section.

Check for Understanding

Books. Use functional words and other vocabulary you have learned to talk about word **libro** (book): **libro en español, libro de casa, libro para usted, libro de Ana** (Ana's book), etc.

Remember that the main noun (**libro**) goes FIRST, followed by the functional word (**de**, etc.) and then the describing noun (**español**, etc.).

Come up with as many examples as you can.

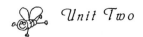

C) TALKING ABOUT SPECIALTY THINGS (optional)

You can use functional words such as **en** / ehn (in, on, at), **para** / PAH-ddah (intended for), and **de** / theh (of, from, about), plus a describing noun, to talk about various kinds of things in your specialty area. Drawing from the "Describing with Nouns ~ Examples," see how many meaningful combinations you can create with the words below. Ask a Spanish speaker to check your work.

_____**en** _____

```
┌─────────────────────────────────────────────────┐
│                                                 │
│                                                 │
│                                                 │
│                                                 │
└─────────────────────────────────────────────────┘
```

_____**para** _____

```
┌─────────────────────────────────────────────────┐
│                                                 │
│                                                 │
│                                                 │
│                                                 │
└─────────────────────────────────────────────────┘
```

_____**de**_____

```
┌─────────────────────────────────────────────────┐
│                                                 │
│                                                 │
│                                                 │
│                                                 │
└─────────────────────────────────────────────────┘
```

_____(con / sin)_____

```
┌─────────────────────────────────────────────────┐
│                                                 │
│                                                 │
│                                                 │
│                                                 │
└─────────────────────────────────────────────────┘
```

_____(y / o)_____

```
┌─────────────────────────────────────────────────┐
│                                                 │
│                                                 │
│                                                 │
└─────────────────────────────────────────────────┘
```

Lesson Three Expressions

mis	meess	my (plural possessions)
sus	sooss	Your, his, her, their (plural possessions)

NOTE: With a child or close friend, native speakers may use the "buddy-buddy" way to say "your," or <u>tu</u>, instead of <u>su</u> (polite "Your"). See the supplemental section for more information.

Speaking Practice

Practice the Lesson Three mini-dialogues using a plural noun (basic or specialty) whenever it would make sense. Add –S or –ES to make the noun plural. If you say "my" or "Your" with a plural noun, be sure to say **mis** and **sus**. Follow the guidelines for "How to Use the Mini-Dialogues" on pages 1-34 and 1-35.

When you see [...], add in "Describing With Nouns" words that make sense. Refer to Lesson Three or your specialty vocabulary for ideas.

NOTE: If you want to talk about two things that are joined with the word "and," as in "my book **and** pen," you say **mi libro y (mi) pluma**, because even though there are two items, you are talking about each one separately. If there is no plural –S on the noun being possessed, there is no –S on **mi** or **su**.

Speaking Activity

Pick a dialogue and act it out. Work with a partner, and use props, if possible.

More Practice

1) Say the Lesson Three "Describing with Nouns ~ Examples" aloud, using the pronunciation guide. Work with a partner if possible.
2) Learn the Lesson Three "Functional Words" and "Describing Nouns" by heart. Study with lists or flashcards.
3) Practice any specialty vocabulary.
4) Visit **www.spanishthatworks.org** for additional suggestions, practice materials, and links to other resources.

Lesson Three Mini-Dialogues:
More About Things

A) Asking about plural possessions

1) (Buenos días / Buenas tardes).	1) (Good morning / afternoon).
2) (Buenos días / Buenas tardes).	2) (Good morning / afternoon).
1) ¿Sus <u>items</u>? *Points.*	1) Your <u>items</u>? *Points.*
2) Sí, mis <u>items</u>.	2) Yes, my <u>items</u>.

B) Requesting a specific item or items

1) (Su / Sus) <u>item(s)</u> [...], por favor.	1) Your <u>item(s)</u> [...], please.
2) Un momento. *Presents item.*	2) One moment. *Presents item.*
1) Gracias. *Takes item.*	1) Thanks. *Takes item.*

C) Giving someone a specific item or items

1) (Mi / Mis) <u>item(s)</u> [...].	1) My <u>item(s)</u> [...].
2) Gracias. *Takes item(s).*	2) Thanks. *Takes item(s).*
1) De nada.	1) You're welcome.

D) When someone forgets an item or items

1) ¡(Señor / Señora / Señorita /Joven)! ¡(Su / sus) <u>item(s)</u> [...]!	1) (Sir / Ma'am / Miss / Young man)! Your <u>item(s)</u> [...]!
2) ¡Ah! ¡Gracias! *Takes item(s).*	2) Oh! Thanks! *Takes item(s).*
1) De nada.	1) You're welcome.

KEY:	(x / y)	Make a choice among words
	<u> </u>	Insert words from your flashcards or word list
	Action	Instructions for role-play
	[...]	Add "Describing With Nouns" words (**en español**, etc.)

EXTRA NOTE:

¿Cómo? / COH-moh means "How?"
but is used when you don't understand or hear
someone, sort of like saying, "Pardon me?"
It's more polite than ¿Qué? / KEH ("What???").

In Mexico, the expression
¿Mande? / MAHN-theh? is also used.

For other useful expressions,
see the "Social Language" portion of the
supplemental section.

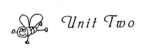

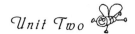

LESSON FOUR: Do you have...?

Basic Structures

A) HOW VERBS CHANGE TO SHOW WHO

This verb is very useful.

tengo	TEHNG-goh	I have
tiene	TYEH-neh	You, s/he, it have
¿Tiene...?	TYEH-neh?	Do You (s/he, it) have?

Spanish verbs change endings to show who is doing the action, so you don't have to say the words for "he," "I," "she," etc.

However, you may wish to use the polite word for "You" (**usted** / oo-sTETH) with a verb, so that the person you are talking to knows that you are speaking directly to him or her, and not talking about someone else, since the verb ending for "You" is the same as for "he," "she," and "it."

Look at these examples.

usted (written abbreviation Ud.)	oo-STETH (oo-STETH)	You (polite)
Usted tiene.	oo-STETH TYEH-neh	You (polite) have.
¿Tiene usted?	TYEH-neh oo-STETH?	Do You (polite) have?

Notice that there is no extra word for "do" in a question. You always use the same verb as in a statement. Just raise your voice at the end of the question, as you do in English. Also notice that Spanish uses a reverse question mark to indicate that a question is about to start.

The English translations of **usted** (You) and **su** (Your) are often capitalized in this text to indicate that you are using the polite form of address. Spanish has a plural **ustedes** (You all or You plural) that is covered in Lesson Seven, plus an intimate or "buddy-buddy" **tú** (you-intimate) and **vosotros** (you all-intimate), that are explained in the supplemental section.

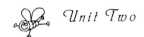

❀❀❀❀❀
Check for Understanding

Items. Say if you have various items, using "Things" words. Use "Describing With Nouns" words when appropriate. Don't respond in a complete sentence.

> Q. ¿Tiene usted <u>item(s) [...]</u>?
> A. Sí. / No.

B) HOW TO SAY NO, NOT, AND DON'T

To make a verb negative, put "no" in front of it.

no (tiene)	noh (<u>T</u>YEH-neh)	(You, s/he, it) don't (have)
¿No (tiene)?	noh (<u>T</u>YEH-neh?)	Don't (You, s/he, it) (have)?
no (tengo)	noh (<u>T</u>EHNG-goh)	(I) don't (have)

"No" also means "no" in answer to a yes / no question. So if someone asks you a yes / no question and you want to say "No, I don't," then you say "no" twice: once to answer the question (No) and once to make the verb negative (don't).

¿Tiene usted?	<u>T</u>YEH-neh oo-STETH?	Do You (polite) have?
No, no tengo.	NOH, noh <u>T</u>EHNG-goh	No, I don't have.

❀❀❀❀❀
Check for Understanding

Do you have? Say if you have an elephant, lion, or tiger. (Answer "No, I don't.")

> Q. ¿Tiene usted un (elefante / león / tigre)?
> A. No, no tengo.

NOTE: The verb is repeated back in this case to convey the two negatives in "No, I do <u>not</u>." It would also be a correct response just to answer "No."

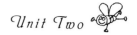

C) HOW TO SAY "A" THING

The Spanish word for "a" (a book, a name, a pen, an address) is related to the counting word for "one" (**uno**).

There are two forms for "a": **un** / oon, and **una** / OO-nah.

People, places, and things all have gender (he or she) in Spanish. "Book" and "name" are "he," or masculine, but "pen" and "address" are "she," or feminine. You use **un** with a masculine word, and **una** with a feminine word. So, **un** libro, **un** nombre, BUT **una** pluma, **una** dirección.

The gender is in the NAME for the thing, not in the thing itself. For instance, "pen" in Spain is **bolígrafo**, which is a "he." "Pen" in Mexico is **pluma**, which is a "she." The gender of something depends on the word a speaker uses.

Nouns (people, places, things) that end in –O are almost always masculine. Nouns that end in –A are usually feminine, though there are a few words you will learn that break this rule.

In your vocabulary lists, nouns ending in –O and –A are not labeled for gender. Nouns ending in something other than –O or –A and exceptions to the rule are labeled (**m.**) for masculine or (**f.**) for feminine. You must memorize the gender for the nouns that don't follow the regular –O and –A pattern.

un	oon	a (one) with a masculine noun
una	OO-nah	a (one) with a feminine noun

Check for Understanding

1) Say **un** or **una** before the "Things" words. Answers in supplemental section.
2) Ask or answer what something is, using the "Things" words.

> Q. ¿Qué es? / KAY-ehss? (What is it?)
> A. (Un / Una) <u>item</u>.

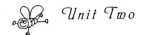

NOTE: IN SPANISH YOU DON'T ALWAYS SAY "A"

As a general rule, Spanish uses **un / una** less than we use "a" in English. **Un / una** really means ONE, so it's often dropped if there is no reason to **count** what you are talking about.

For example, in English you say, "I'm <u>a</u> student," but unless you want to emphasize that you are unique or only "one," in Spanish it's simply "I'm student" (**Soy estudiante** / soy eh-s<u>t</u>oo-th'YAHN-<u>t</u>eh).

Also, when Spanish speakers say that they DON'T HAVE (a) thing, they often leave out **un / una**. So you might hear **No tengo problema**, which translates as "I don't have (-) problem." Remember, **un / una** means "one." If you don't have something, why count it?

For now, the important thing is to learn how to say **un / una** and to be aware that sometimes native speakers leave it out.

Lesson Four Expressions

Sí.	see	Yes.
No.	noh	No. (to yes/no question)
no (+ a verb)	noh	not / don't (+ a verb)
¡Cómo no!	COH-moh NOH	Of course! (how not!)
¡Claro!	CLAH-ddoh	Of course! (clearly!)
Lo siento.	loh s'YEHN-<u>t</u>oh	I'm sorry.
Ah, bueno.	ah BWEH-noh	Oh, okay (good).
pero	PEHddoh	but
Hay... ¿Hay?	"AYE"	There is, There are, Is there? Are there?
No hay.	noh "AYE"	There isn't, aren't
mañana	mahn-YAH-nah	tomorrow

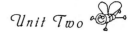

Speaking Practice

Practice the Lesson Four mini-dialogues, using your "Things" words (basic or specialty) for the <u>item</u> blanks. Work with a partner, if possible.
1) For dialogue A, partner # 1 should go in the order of the "Things" flashcards or list. Partner # 2 can respond with any other noun.
2) For dialogues B and C, partner #2 has the option of saying yes or no. Partner #1 should use a response that makes sense.
3) For dialogue C, you can use **¿Tiene?** (do You have?) or **¿Hay?** /AYE (are there?) to ask if items are available.
4) Redo dialogues A and B, making all the "Things" plural. <u>Don't</u> make **un / una** plural—just leave it out. (The plural forms **unos / unas** ("some") are not required, and often omitted, so keep it simple for now). However, <u>do</u> change **mi** to **mis** and **su** to **sus** if there is more than one thing being possessed.

Use Lesson Three "Describing With Nouns" words when appropriate.

Speaking Activities

1) Pick a dialogue and act it out. Work with a partner, and use props, if possible.
2) Write a dialogue based on the Lesson Four mini-dialogues, and use ONLY the vocabulary presented in this lesson and previous lessons. Write out one version of the original dialogue, and then modify it slightly by reorganizing it in a creative way or adding an expression from another dialogue.

Do NOT write a dialogue in English and translate it. If you can be creative with a limited number of words and structures, you will learn to think in Spanish. Also, the point is to practice the words in the lesson. If you are in a class, stick to the material in the lessons, so all your classmates can understand you.

3) Act out your own dialogue. Work with a partner, and use props, if possible.

More Practice

1) Say the Lesson Four structures and expressions aloud, using the guide. Work with a partner if you can. Make flashcards or a study list.
2) Learn the Lesson Four structures and expressions by heart.
3) Optional: review "Social Language" words, starting on page S-11 of the supplemental section. Practice any specialty words.
4) Visit **www.spanishthatworks.org** for additional suggestions, practice materials, and links to other resources.

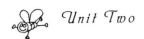

Lesson Four Mini-Dialogues:
Do you have…?

A) Asking for one thing & getting something else

1) ¿Tiene (un / una) <u>item</u>?	1) Do You have an <u>item</u>?
2) No, pero tengo (un / una) <u>item</u>.	2) No, but I have an <u>item</u>.
1) (Ah, bueno. / Lo siento.)	1) (Oh, okay. / I'm sorry.)

B) Asking if someone has something

1) ¿Tiene (su / mi/ un / una) <u>item</u>?	1) Do You have (Your / my /an) <u>item</u>?

2) Sí, cómo no. Un momento.	2) Yes, of course. One moment.
OR	
2) No, no tengo. Lo siento. *Shakes head.*	2) No, I don't. I'm sorry. *Shakes head.*

1) (Gracias. / Ah, bueno.)	1) (Thanks. / Oh, okay.)

C) Asking if things are available

1) (Señor / Señora / Señorita /Joven), ¿(tiene / hay) <u>items</u>?	1) (Sir / Ma'am / Miss / Young man), (do You have / are there any) <u>items</u>?

2) Sí, claro. *Presents item(s).*	2) Yes, of course. *Presents item(s).*
OR	
2) No, (no tengo / no hay). *Shakes head.*	2) No, (I don't have / there aren't any). *Shakes head.*

1) (Gracias. / Bueno, mañana. / Lo siento.)	1) (Thanks. / Okay, tomorrow. / I'm sorry.)

EXTRA NOTE:

¿Hay? / AYE (Is or are there?)
is useful in public places, when you just want to
know if something is available.

For example, to use the telephone, you can say
¿Hay teléfono? (Is there a phone?)

¿Tiene teléfono? (Do <u>You</u> have a phone?)
is more personal, because you are asking a person
directly if he or she <u>has</u> something.

UNIT THREE:

"Where is it?
It's over there!"

Lesson 5: Where is / are...?

- ❖ The Four Ways to Say "The"
- ❖ How Verbs Show Plural (-N): Is / Are Located
- ❖ Expressions (Excuse me, where?, here, look...)
- ❖ Mini-Dialogues

Lesson 6: Places

- ❖ Basic Places
- ❖ Specialty Places
- ❖ Describing Places
- ❖ Expressions (Well, near...)
- ❖ Mini-Dialogues

LESSON FIVE: Where is / are...?

Basic Structures

A) THE FOUR WAYS TO SAY "THE"

The Spanish word for "the" (the book, the pen, the books, the pens) has four different forms. The form depends on whether the noun is masculine or feminine, singular or plural. You learned how to make nouns plural in Lesson Three, and you learned about masculine and feminine nouns in Lesson Four.

SINGULAR

The two singular forms for "the" are **el** and **la**.

el	ehl	the (with "masculine" noun)
la	lah	the (with "feminine" noun)

So, **el libro** (the book), **el nombre** (the name), but **la pluma** (the pen), **la dirección** (the address).

PLURAL

The plural for **el** is <u>los</u>, and the plural for **la** is <u>las</u>.

los	lohs	the (with plural "masculine" noun)
las	lahs	the (with plural "feminine" noun)

So, **los libros** (the books), **los nombres** (the names), but **las plumas** (the pens), **las direcciones** (the addresses).

For the most part, "the" is used in Spanish just as in English, to refer to some SPECIFIC thing, which implies that both people in the conversation know what is being talked about. For example, **la clase** (the class) is the one we all know about, while **una clase** (a class) is an unspecified one.

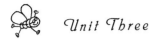

However, Spanish <u>does</u> use **el / la / los / las** in cases of abstract or general nouns, when English would not use "the." For example, in English we can say "Life is beautiful," but in Spanish you say <u>La</u> **vida es bella** ("The" life is beautiful).

Another example is when you are speaking **about** another person, and using a title such as Mr. or Mrs. In this case, you use the word "the" before the title. Title words can be used with or without proper names.

Examples:

El señor García está en la oficina.	"The" Mr. Garcia is in the office.
La señora Jiménez tiene la pluma.	"The" Mrs. Jimenez has the pen.
La señorita no tiene papel.	The young lady doesn't have paper.

NOTE: You do NOT use "the" with a title word when addressing someone directly.

Examples:

¡Buenos días, señor!	Good morning, sir!
Buenas tardes, señora Jiménez.	Good afternoon, Mrs. Jimenez.
¿Tiene lápiz, señorita?	Do you have (a) pencil, Miss?

Remember that "a" is sometimes left out in Spanish. This means that Spanish uses "a" a little bit less, and "the" a little bit more, than English.

Note also that Spanish also uses capital letters less than English does. This is something to be aware of as you are learning Spanish.

Check for Understanding

Ways to say "the." 1) Go through your "Basic Things" words, choosing **el** or **la** for each word. Check your responses with the answer key in the supplemental section. Then practice saying **el** or **la** with any "Specialty Things" words.
2) Go through the basic and specialty "Things" words again, this time making each noun plural and choosing **los** or **las** for each word. Check your responses for the "Basic Things" words with the answer key in the supplemental section.
3) Use your basic or specialty "Things" flashcards and a list to play a game. One partner secretly draws a card. The other partner uses the list to guess what the other partner has chosen. Players count the number of right guesses. To make it easier, allow three guesses per flashcard. Follow this dialogue. Be sure to pause after the word "no," so it means "no," instead of "don't."

Q. ¿Tiene (el / la) <u>item</u>?

A1. Sí.

OR

A2. No. (Pause). Tengo (el / la) <u>different item</u>.

B) HOW VERBS SHOW 3ʳᵈ PERSON PLURAL (-N)

Look at these Spanish verbs:

está	eh-S<u>T</u>AH	is located
están	eh-S<u>T</u>AHN	are located

As you can see, you add an –N to talk about more than one object or person. You may think of it this way: –S shows plural for nouns, but –N shows plural for verbs.

Examples:

El libro está aquí.	The book is (located) here.
Los libros están aquí.	The books are (located) here.
La pluma está allá.	The pen is (located) over there.
Las plumas están allá.	The pens are (located) over there.

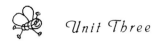

❀❀❀❀❀❀
Check for Understanding

Here & There

1) **Drill.** Say BOTH of the following statements for EACH item of your "Things" words. Remember to add –S or –ES to the item for the second statement. Say the statements with a singsong rhythm and really STRESS the last syllable in **está**, **están**, **aquí**, and **allá**. Focus on the sounds of the words and on creating the plurals, rather than on the real meaning of the statements.

(El / La) <u>item</u> está aquí / ah-KEE.

AND

(Los / Las) <u>items</u> están allá / ah-YAH.

2) **Communicate.** Now, make meaningful statements about items in the room: "The book is here," "the table (**la mesa** / lah MEH-sah) is over there," etc.

Lesson Five Expressions

Perdón.	pai*rr*-THOHN	Excuse me/ Sorry.
¿Dónde?	THOHN-theh (muffled th sound)	Where?
¿Dónde está / están?	THOHN-theh eh-S<u>T</u>AH / eh S<u>T</u>AHN?	Where is / are?
aquí	ah-KEE	here
allá	ah-YAH	over there
en	ehn	in, on, at a location
No sé.	noh-SEH	I don't know.
Mire.	MEEddeh	Look! (See.)
De nada	theh NAH-thah	You're welcome.
Gracias a usted.	g'DDAH-s'yahss ah oo-STETH	Thank <u>you</u>. (Instead of You're welcome)
¿Aló?	ah-LOH?	Hello? (phone L. America)
¿Bueno?	BWEH-noh?	Hello? (phone Mexico)
soy	soy	I am ("This is" so-and-so on the phone)
No está.	noh eh-S<u>T</u>AH	S/he is not in.
Adiós.	ah-th'YOHSS	Good-bye.

Speaking Practice

Practice the Lesson Five mini-dialogues. Work with a partner, if possible.

1) In the dialogues with "Things" words, you may add "Describing With Nouns" words from Lesson Three after the "Things" word(s).

2) In English, the "Look!" in dialogue B sounds abrupt. **Mire**, however, is a polite command in Spanish, and is used frequently to get someone's attention. **Mire** can translate as "See?," "Excuse me," or even a "filler" word such as "Well...." You may have already heard the "buddy-buddy" form **mira / MEEddah**, which is appropriate to say to a child, close friend, or family member.

3) In dialogues B & C, Partner #2 has a choice of how to respond.

4) For dialogue C, use the list of names given, or names of people you know.

Speaking Activities

1) Pick a dialogue and act it out. Work with a partner, and use props, if possible.

2) Write a dialogue based on the Lesson Five mini-dialogues, and use ONLY the vocabulary presented in this lesson and previous lessons.

3) Act out your own dialogue. Work with a partner, and use props, if possible.

More Practice

1) Practice saying the Lesson Five structures and expressions aloud, using the guide. Work with a partner if you can. Make flashcards or a study list.

2) Learn the Lesson Five structures and expressions by heart.

3) Begin reviewing verbs you have learned. Review any specialty words.

4) Visit **www.spanishthatworks.org** for additional suggestions, practice materials, and links to other resources.

Lesson Five Mini-Dialogues:
Where is / are...?

A) Someone brings something to you

1) (Buenos días / Buenas tardes). Aquí está (el / la) <u>item</u> [...]. *Presents item.*	1) (Good morning / afternoon). Here is (the) <u>item</u> [...]. *Presents item.*
2) Gracias. *Takes item.*	2) Thanks. *Takes item.*
1) Gracias a usted.	1) Thank <u>you.</u>

B) Someone asks where things are

1) Perdón, ¿dónde están (los / las) <u>items</u> [...]?	1) Excuse me, where are (the) <u>items</u> [...]?
2) (Aquí / Allá), mire. *Indicates direction.*	2) (Here / Over there), look (see). *Indicates direction.*
OR	
2) No sé. Un momento, por favor.	2) I don't know. One moment, please.
1) Ah bueno. Gracias.	1) Oh, okay. Thanks.

C) Asking if someone is in

1) *Phone rings.* (¿Aló? / ¿Bueno?)	1) *Phone rings.* (Hello? / Hello?-Mex.)
2) (Buenos días / Buenas tardes). Soy _____. *(Say your name.)* ¿Está _____, por favor?	2) Hello. (Formal greeting) This is _____. *(Say your name.)* Is _____ in, please?
1) Sí, un momento.	1) Yes, one moment.
OR	
1) No, lo siento. No está.	1) No, I'm sorry. S/he isn't in.
2) (Gracias. / Ah, gracias. Adiós)	2) (Thanks. / Oh, thanks. Good-bye.)

NAMES: Luis Villa, Verónica García, David Flores, Elena Padilla, la señora López, la señorita Castro, el señor Paz, la señora Vásquez, OTHER

EXTRA NOTE:

Some Spanish textbooks use **el** and **la** before the noun to indicate the gender of the word. For example, a word list might indicate that the way to say "pencil" is **el lápiz**.

El lápiz, however, really means "**the** pencil."

This is important, because if you want to say "a pencil" (**un lápiz**) or "my pencil" (**mi lápiz**), you drop the **el** ("the"), because it doesn't make sense to say "the" in those cases.

Spanish that Works uses the symbols (m.) for masculine and (f.) for feminine to indicate gender whenever the noun ending does not follow the pattern of **–O** (masculine) and **–A** (feminine).

LESSON SIX: Places

A) BASIC PLACES

entrada	ehn-t'DDAH-thah	entrance
salida	sah-LEE-thah	exit
sala	SAH-lah	public room, living room
coche (m.)	COH-cheh	car
tienda	T'YEHN-thah	store, shop
mesa	MEH-sah	table, table-like desk
oficina	oh-fee-SEE-nah	office
área (f.) (el área)	AHdday-ah	area
piso (uno, dos, tres...)	PEE-soh (OO-noh, thohss, t'ddehs)	floor (#1, 2, 3...)
baño	BAHN-yoh	bathroom
casa	CAH-sah	house, home
calle (f.)	CAH-yeh	street, "outside"

NOTES:

Some speakers prefer the word **salón** (m.) / sah-LOHN instead of **sala** (f.) for a public room, depending on dialect and on context.

To talk about numbered floors, you can use a cardinal number (one, two, three, etc.) after the word "floor." So "the eighth floor" is **el piso ocho**. (For other numbers, visit www.spanishthatworks.org for a reference sheet or see pages 7-4 and 7-5. Spanish speakers may use ordinal numbers for the "first floor" (**primer piso**), "second floor" (**segundo piso**), and "third floor" (**tercer piso**). However, if you use **piso uno**, **piso dos**, and **piso tres**, you will be understood.

In some countries, the "first" floor is the floor <u>above</u> the main floor. The main floor is then called **planta baja** /PLAHN-tah BAH-hah or **piso de entrada**. Use the expression "this floor" (**este piso** / EH-steh PEE-soh) if you need to clarify.

More floor words

piso principal (m.)	ehl PEE-soh p'ddeen-see-PAHL	main floor
en este piso	ehn EH-steh PEE-soh	on this floor
sótano	SOH-tah-noh	basement

B) SPECIALTY PLACES (optional)

Refer to, or make up, a list of additional <u>places</u> words (locations, or places in which items may be kept), that are essential for communication in your specialty area. You may ask your teacher or visit **www.spanishthatworks.org** for ideas. If you use a dictionary, make sure each word is a noun (person, place or thing) and note the noun's gender (**m.** or **f.**). Look up the word on the Spanish side of the dictionary to double-check the translation or to find the gender.

Make up a pronunciation guide for your specialty words, using the chart at the beginning of Unit One. Then fill out this blank chart with the twelve most important specialty words. Some may overlap with the basic words. You may also wish to use or make up specialty word flashcards.

SPANISH	PRONUNCIATION	ENGLISH

✿✾✿✾✿
Check for Understanding

Places Words.   1) Practice saying the "Places" words, both basic and specialty, until you are familiar with them. Follow the three steps in "How to Practice Vocabulary" outlined in Lesson Two.

2) Practice saying "the" (**el** or **la**) with the "Places" words. If the word does not follow the regular pattern of –**O** ending for a masculine word and –**A** ending for a feminine word, the correct gender will be indicated by (m.) or (f.).

NOTE: The word **área** (f.) is special. Although it is feminine, you say **el** in the singular. So, it is **el área**, but **las areas**. This is true for some other words starting with an **a** / ah sound, such as **agua** (f.), which means "water." You say **el agua**, but **las aguas**.

You will not use **el** or **la** with places words such as **aquí** (here), **afuera** / ah-FWEH-ddah (outside), and **cerca de** (near), because these words are not nouns.

C) DESCRIBING PLACES

You can use the functional words (**en, para, por, de, con, sin, y, o**) plus another noun to talk about places. In fact, some "Places" words already have describing nouns built into them.

Look at these words. All are nouns.

clase (f.)	CLAH-seh	class
junta	HOON-tah	meeting
conferencia	cohn-fehDDEHN s'yah	conference
hombre (m.)	OHM-b'ddeh	man
mujer (f.)	moo-HAIRR	woman
arte (m.)	AHRR-teh	art
música	MOO-see-cah	music

With the functional words and other nouns, you can create all sorts of combinations. Let's take the word **sala**, for example, which is one way to say "public room."

You can talk about **la sala de clase** (the classroom), **la sala de junta** (the meeting room), **la sala de música** (the music room), **la sala de conferencia** (the conference room), **la sala de arte** (the art room), and so forth.

The article ("a" or "the") goes with the main noun, which is the noun you say first. So, let's say you are using the word **salón** (m.) / sah-LOHN for a public room, instead of **sala**. Even though the nouns **clase** and **junta** are feminine, they are part of the describing phrase, and not the main noun. So, you say <u>el</u> **salón de clase** and <u>el</u> **salón de junta** because <u>salón</u> is masculine. You also say <u>el</u> **coche de <u>la</u> señora Villa** (Mrs. Villa's car) and <u>la</u> **oficina d<u>el</u> señor Villa** (Mr. Villa's office) because the main nouns are "car" (<u>el</u> coche) and "office" (<u>la</u> oficina).

Remember that in Spanish, you can't put a describing noun in front of another noun. So that's why "the meeting room" is really "the room of meeting." To indicate specific kinds of rooms, offices, etc. you will usually use **de** / theh (of, from, belonging to). However, **para** / PAHddah will sometimes express the same general meaning as **de**. For example, **baño de mujeres** (women's bathroom) and **baño para mujeres** (bathroom for women) both express the same idea.

Please note that you usually leave out the word **de** /theh if you describe a place with a proper name or a number. For example, to say "The Saguaro Room," you would put the name "Saguaro" <u>after</u> the word "room," and <u>without</u> a functional word: **El Salón Saguaro**. To say "Room 8-B," you would also put the number <u>after</u> the word "room," and <u>without</u> a functional word: **Sala 8-B** / SAH-lah OH-choh BEH. (For more numbers, see Lesson Thirteen, pages 7-4 and 7-5, or get the reference sheet at **www.spanishthatworks.org**.)

You can mix and match "Places" words to create all sorts of combinations.

Examples:

el área de trabajo	the work area
el trabajo de usted	Your work (or workplace)
la tienda de música	the music store
la entrada de la tienda	the store entrance
la música en la calle	the music on the street
la calle Ocho	8th Street

Check for Understanding

Kinds of Places. 1) Translate to Spanish, using vocabulary from this lesson.

1) the classroom

2) the computer area
(area of computers)

3) the women's bathroom
(bathroom of women)

4) "the" Room 8-B

5) the table at (in) the entrance

6) the Lewis & Clark Room

7) the bathroom for men
("of" men also works)

8) the office of "the" Mrs. Padilla

2) **More Combinations.** See what other sorts of combinations you can make, using your "Places" words plus other vocabulary, such as your "Things" words. Remember to put the main noun first, then the functional word, and then the describing noun. Omit the functional word with a proper name or number.

_____ de _____   _____ en _____

_____ para _____   _____ con _____

Lesson Six Expressions

Pues...	PWEHSS	Well...so...then
cerca de	SAIRR-cah theh	near (to)
Sígame	SEE-gah-meh	Follow me
Mexico	MAY-hee-coh	Mexico
banco	BAHN-coh	bank (for money)

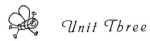
 ### Speaking Practice

Make a separate list or flashcards for the "Places" words (basic or specialty). As you practice the Lesson Six mini-dialogues, you will first the word list provided and then improvise from your list or flashcards. Work with a partner, if possible.

1) For the sake of practice, everything you ask about in dialogue A will be either near the entrance or the bank. For dialogue B, use your "Things" flashcards, and the list of places given. You can improvise with other "Places" words from your list or flashcards.

2) Try to use "Describing" words from Lessons Three and Six with your "Things" words. For example, to talk about **el papel**, you can say:

> el papel para la junta, el papel de la conferencia, el papel del* baño,
> el papel para las computadoras, el papel de la señora Jiménez, etc.

> *NOTE: The word **del** is a contraction without apostrophe of **de + el**.

3) For dialogue C, use the list of names, or names of people you know. Partner #2 has the choice of telling where the person is, or saying that he or she doesn't know. You can substitute other place names for **México**. To say that someone is "not here," you do not use the word **aquí**. Just say **No está**.

Speaking Activities

1) Pick a dialogue and act it out. Work with a partner, and use props, if possible.

2) Write a new dialogue based on the Lesson Six mini-dialogues and use ONLY the vocabulary presented in this lesson and previous lessons. If you can, incorporate new "Describing Places" words from Lesson Six.

3) Act out your own dialogue. Work with a partner, and use props, if possible.

More Practice

1) Practice saying your "Places" words (basic and specialty), the "Describing Places" words, and the Lesson Six expressions aloud, using the pronunciation guide. Work with a partner if possible. Make flashcards or study lists.

2) Learn the "Places" words (basic and specialty), the "Describing Places" words, and the Lesson Six expressions by heart.

3) Visit **www.spanishthatworks.org** for additional suggestions, practice materials, and links to other resources.

Lesson Six Mini-Dialogues:
Places

A) Asking where places are

1) Perdón, ¿dónde está (el / la) <u>place</u>?	1) Excuse me, where is the <u>place</u>?
2) Pues, (aquí / allá), mire. Cerca de (la entrada / el banco). *Indicates direction.*	2) Well, (here / over there), see. Near (the entrance / the bank). *Indicates direction.*
1) Gracias.	1) Thanks.
2) De nada.	2) You're welcome

PLACES: la sala de clase, la sala de junta, el área de las computadoras, la oficina, el baño de mujeres, el baño de hombres, el coche, OTHER

B) Asking where something is

1) ¿Dónde está (el / la) <u>item</u>?	1) Where is the <u>item</u>?
2) En (el / la) <u>place</u>.	2) In the <u>place</u>.
1) ¿Dónde?	1) Where?
2) (Pues, aquí, mire. / Sígame, por favor.)	2) (Well, here, look. / Follow me, please.)

PLACES FOR THINGS: mi casa, la mesa, la sala de clase, mi coche, el banco, la oficina, la sala 8-B, el piso ocho, la basura / bah-SOO-ddah (trash), OTHER

C) Asking where someone is

1) ¿Dónde está _____?	1) Where is _____?
2) Está en (casa / la oficina / el baño / el trabajo / México).	2) S/he is in/at (home / the office / the bathroom / work / Mexico).
OR	
2) No sé. No está.	2) I don't know. S/he is not in.

NAMES: Miguel, Teresa, Julia, Guadalupe, Fernando, la señora Flores, OTHER

EXTRA NOTE:

English speakers often make the mistake of using the word **a** / ah (to) to give location, because **a** / ah (to) is used to express things that are happening **at** a certain time.

However, to give a location, you need to use the word **en** / ehn (in, on, at, within, inside). So, "at home" is **en casa**, "at school" is **en la escuela**, and "at work" is **en el trabajo**.

For now, it may help you to think of **en** as the "location preposition." You will very often use **en** with **está** and **están**.

UNIT FOUR:

"My friend needs a pen or a pencil."

Lesson 7:   Need & Want

- ❖ The Plural-N Again (I, You, s/he, You all, they need)
- ❖ You and You all
- ❖ Want (I, You, s/he, You all, they want)
- ❖ Specialty Things to Need or Want
- ❖ Expressions (What?, help, very well, nothing...)
- ❖ Mini-Dialogues

Lesson 8:   People

- ❖ Family Words (Mom, dad, children...)
- ❖ Specialty People Words: (Job titles, etc.)
- ❖ Expressions (All right, let's go, now...)
- ❖ Mini-Dialogues

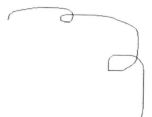

LESSON SEVEN: I need...

Basic Structures

A) THE PLURAL –N AGAIN

Look at these Spanish verbs:

tengo / ¿tengo?	TEHNG-goh	I have / do I have?
tiene ¿tiene?	TYEH-neh	You, s/he, it have or has do You s/he have?
tienen ¿tienen?	TYEH-nehn	You all, they have do You all, they have?

necesito	neh-seh-SEE-toh	I need
necesita ¿necesita?	neh-seh-SEE-tah	You, s/he, it need do You, s/he need?
necesitan ¿necesitan?	neh-seh-SEE-tahn	You all, they need do You all, they need?

Spanish verb endings show **person**, or <u>who</u> is doing the action. In present tense verbs, the –O ending means "I." The –E and –A endings mean one person (singular): "You polite," "she," "he," or "it." The –N ending means more than one person (plural): "You all" or "they."

Remember, with Spanish nouns (both people and things) the –O ending usually means masculine, and the –A ending usually means feminine.

However, there are NO masculine or feminine verbs in Spanish. The present tense –O ending means "I" for either a man or a woman. The –A ending is used for both "he" and "she." Spanish nouns (and adjectives) have gender, but Spanish verbs do not.

NOTE: In this course, you will not actively practice the "we" form of verbs such as "have" and "need," because the "we" verbs are long, and sometimes different from the other forms. In conversation you can usually convey the idea of a "we" verb (such as "we have") by using an "I" verb ("I have") or a "s/he" verb ("the class has"). This greatly simplifies the verb endings and makes it easier for you to start speaking Spanish.

For more information about the "we" form, see the supplemental section.

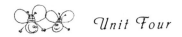

B) YOU and YOU ALL

You have learned that Spanish verbs change endings to show who is doing the action, so you don't have to say "I," "he," "she," etc.

However, just as the polite word for "You" (**usted**) is often used when speaking to one person, the plural word for "You" (**ustedes**) is used when speaking to a group, so that people know you are speaking directly to them, and not talking about others. In this text, the plural "You" (**ustedes**) will be referred to as "You all," but you can substitute "You plural" (or "You guys / girls") if you prefer.

ustedes (may be written **Uds.**)	oo-STEH-thehss	You all (You pl.)
¿necesitan ustedes?	neh-seh-SEE-tahn oo-STEH-thehss?	do You all need?

NOTE: Remember that the word **su** (or **sus**, when a plural object is being possessed) can mean **Your, his, her, its,** and **their**.

The word **su** always agrees with the number of things possessed, and not with the number of owners. So, "They have their book" is **Tienen su libro**. "He has his books" is **Tiene sus libros**. Remember, no plural –S on the noun, no –S on **su**.

Check for Understanding

Has & Needs. Use the text to translate these verbs into Spanish. Do **NOT** say the Spanish words for **he, she, I,** or **they**. **DO** say the Spanish words for **You** and **You all** (usted / ustedes), plus specifics such as **the class** (la clase).

1) I need

2) They need

3) You have

4) You all need

5) She needs

6) He has

7) The class has

8) I have

9) You all have

10) He needs

11) Margarita needs

12) They have

13) You need

14) She has

C) WANT

The verb "want" may be used similarly to "need."

quiero	k'YEHddoh	I want
quiere	k'YEHddeh	You, s/he want
quieren	k'YEHddehn	You all, they want

This verb "want" is easy to say, but it causes difficulties because the Spanish "qui" is pronounced like the English word "key," and NOT like the English "qui" of "require." Remember it this way: The <u>key</u> to life is knowing what you <u>want</u>.

key-YEHddoh (k'YEHddoh) = I want
key-YEHddeh (k'YEHddeh) = You, s/he want
key-YEHddehn (k'YEHddehn) = You all, they want

Latinos often use the more polite form **quisiera** / kee-s'YEHddah (I'd like), instead of **quiero** (I want), when requesting things from others. It can also sound more polite to use **necesito** (I need), when asking for something.

Quiero, quiere, quieren also mean "love" when talking about people. So, "I love my family" is **Quiero a mi familia.** (NOTE: Spanish always adds the word **a** / ah (to) when the action is happening **to people**.)

To talk about a <u>thing</u> that you like or "love," you may use the expression **me gusta** / may GOO-s<u>t</u>ah, which literally means "it pleases me." If you like more than one thing, you say **me gustan** (they are pleasing to me). So, "I like (the) Spanish" is **Me gusta el español.** "I like (the) books" is **Me gustan los libros.**

D) SPECIALTY THINGS TO NEED OR WANT (optional)

Refer to, or make up, a list of additional <u>items</u> in your specialty area that one may <u>have</u>, <u>need</u> or <u>want</u>. If you use a dictionary, make sure each word is a noun (person, place or thing) and note the noun's gender (**m.** or **f.**). Look up the word on the Spanish side of the dictionary to double-check the translation or to find the gender. Ask your teacher or visit **www.spanishthatworks.org** for additional ideas.

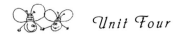

Make up a pronunciation guide for your specialty words, using the "Saying & Understanding" chart at the beginning of Unit One. Then fill out this blank chart with the twelve most important words. Some may overlap with the basic words. You may also wish to use or make up specialty word flashcards.

You may study or review your specialty vocabulary using the steps outlined in "How to Practice Vocabulary" from Lesson Two.

SPANISH	PRONUNCIATION	ENGLISH

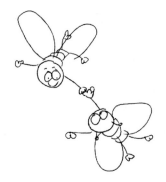

Check for Understanding

Want, etc. 1) Translate these sentences, using **quiero**, **quiere**, or **quieren**.

1) I want a book in Spanish, please.

2) Do You want a pencil?

3) They want more.

4) Do You all (pl.) want help?

5) I don't want anything ("nothing").

6) My mom (**mi mamá** / mee mah-MAH) wants a pen.

2) **Sentences.** Make or obtain flashcards for the verbs "have," "need," and "want" and use them with your "Things" flashcards (basic or specialty) to make up simple sentences. Use the articles "a" and "the" as necessary. You may also use the word **más** / MAHSS (more) when appropriate. Examples:

Tengo una pluma.	I have a pen.
¿Necesita una pluma?	Do You need a pen?
Quiero más papel.	I want more paper.

Lesson Seven Expressions

¿Qué?	keh?	What?
ayuda	ah-YOO-thah	help (noun)
Hola, buenos días / Hola, buenas tardes.	OH-lah (etc.)	Hello ("hola" by itself is more informal, like "hi")
Muy bien	mooy b'YEHN	Very well.
Por aquí.	POHddah-KEE	This way. (direction)
eso	EH-soh	that (unspecified thing)
nada	NAH-thah	nothing
todo	TOH-thoh	everything, all
más	MAHSS	more
¿Qué más?	keh MAHSS?	What else?
¿Algo más?	AHL-goh MAHSS?	Something else?
Nada más.	NAH-thah MAHSS	Nothing else.
Es todo.	ehss TOH-thoh	That's all.
ya	YAH	already
amigo, amiga	ah-MEE-goh / ah-MEE-gah	friend (m.), friend (f.)

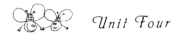

 Speaking Practice

1) Practice the Lesson Seven mini-dialogues, using your "Things" list or flashcards or other specialty nouns.
2) Go through the mini-dialogues a second time, substituting the verb "want" for the verb "need."

NOTE: When you are talking about MORE of something, some words will need to be made plural, and some won't. Go by what make sense in English. For example, in English, you would say "more book**s**" in the plural, but "more money" in the singular. Spanish is usually the same: **más libros** (more books), but **más dinero** / thee-NEHddoh (more money).

Speaking Activities

1) Pick a dialogue and act it out. Work with a partner, and use props, if possible.
2) Write a dialogue based on the Lesson Seven mini-dialogues, and use ONLY the vocabulary presented in this lesson and previous lessons.
3) Act out your own dialogue. Work with a partner, and use props, if possible.

More Practice

1) Practice saying the Lesson Seven structures and expressions aloud, using the pronunciation guide. Work with a partner if you can.
2) Learn by heart the Lesson Seven structures and expressions, as well as all other verbs you have studied up to this point. Make study lists or flashcards.
3) Practice any specialty vocabulary from this lesson.
4) Visit **www.spanishthatworks.org** for additional suggestions, practice materials, and links to other resources.

Lesson Seven Mini-Dialogues:
I need...

A) Asking someone what he or she needs

1) ¿Qué necesita?	1) What do You need?
2) Necesito (mi / su / un / una) <u>item</u>, por favor.	2) I need (my / Your / an) <u>item</u>, please.
1) Muy bien. ¿Qué más?	1) Very well. What else?
2) Nada más.	2) Nothing else.

B) Asking for what you need

1) Hola, buenos días. Necesito (mi / su / un / una) <u>item</u>.	1) Hello. I need (my / Your / an) <u>item</u>.
2) Eso está en (la sala de clase / la oficina / OTHER). ¿Algo más?	2) That's in (the classroom / the office / OTHER). Anything else?
1) No, gracias. Es todo.	1) No, thanks. That's all.

C) Asking if someone needs help

1) ¿Necesita ayuda?	1) Do You need help?

2) Sí, necesito más <u>item</u>(s).	2) Yes, I need more <u>item</u>(s).
OR	
2) No, gracias. Ya tengo mi <u>item</u>.	2) No, thanks. I already have my <u>item</u>.

D) Asking people in a group if they need help-one replies

1) ¿Necesitan ayuda?	1) Do You all need help?
2) Sí, mis amigos necesitan más <u>item</u>(s).	2) Yes, my friends need more <u>item</u>(s).
1) Muy bien. Por aquí, por favor.	1) Very well. This way, please.

EXTRA NOTE:

In Mexico and other parts of Latin America, politeness with language is highly valued, especially in customer service situations.

One way to be polite in Spanish is to use **quisiera** / kee-s'YEHddah (I'd like), instead of the more direct **quiero** / k'YEHddoh (I want).

When someone has been helpful, Latinos may use the expression **Es usted muy amable** / ehss oo-STETH mooy ah-MAH-bleh (You are very kind).

LESSON EIGHT: People Words

A) FAMILY WORDS

familia	fah-MEEL-yah	family
mamá	mah-MAH	mom
papá (m.)	pah-PAH	dad
padres (m. pl.)	PAH-th'ddehss	parents
niño / niña	NEEN-yoh / NEEN-yah	boy / girl
niños	NEEN-yohss	children (anyone's)
hijo / hija	EE-hoh / EE-hah	son / daughter
hijos	EE-hohss	children (your own)
esposo / esposa	eh-SPOH-soh / -sah	husband / wife
hermano / hermana	ai*rr*-MAH-noh / -nah	brother / sister
novio / novia	NOH-v'yoh / NOH-v'yah	boyfriend / girlfriend (romantic)
amigo / amiga	ah-MEE-goh / ah-MEE-gah	friend (m.) / friend (f). (platonic)

You may have learned **madre** / MAH-th'ddeh (mother) and **padre** / PAH-th'ddeh (father), instead of "mom" and "dad." However, in many Latin American countries, **madre** is used in vulgar expressions, so **mamá** (and **papá**) are preferred, especially after **my** and **your**.

The words **hijos** and **niños** both translate as "children." However, **hijos** are offspring (sons and daughters), while **niños** are just children in general.

You may also have heard the expressions **m'hijo** / MEE-hoh and **m'hija** / MEE-hah, which are commonly used in Mexico and several other Spanish-speaking countries. These expressions come from "my child" (**mi hijo, mi hija**), and are used affectionately when addressing children, sort of like saying "dear."

The words **novia** and **novio** can also mean "bride" and "groom," and are only used for romantic relationships. For platonic friendships, use the words **amiga** and **amigo**.

For an <u>all female</u> group, you add –S (–AS if the word ends in a consonant) to the feminine singular form. So, "daughters" are **hijas**, and "sisters" are **hermanas**.

To express EITHER an <u>all male</u> OR a male and female <u>mixed</u> group, you add –S (–ES if the word ends in a consonant) to the male form. **Hijos** can mean "sons" or "sons and daughters." **Hermanos** can mean "brothers" or "siblings."

In many people words, the masculine form ends in –O, and the related feminine form ends in –A. So, **niño** / NEEN-yoh is "boy," and **niña** / NEEN-yah is "girl." A male teacher is **maestro** / my-EHSS-<u>t</u>'ddoh, while a female teacher is **maestra** / my-EHSS-<u>t</u>'ddah. The plurals are **maestros** and **maestras**.

For the people words that end in –E, only the article ("a" or "the") changes to show male versus female. So "the boy student" is <u>el</u> **estudiante** / ehl eh-s<u>t</u>oo-th'YAHN-teh, but "the girl student" is <u>la</u> **estudiante** / lah eh-s<u>t</u>oo-th'YAHN-<u>t</u>eh. The plural form is **estudiantes**.

The word **bebé** / beh-BEH, or "baby," which was borrowed from the English, follows a similar pattern: <u>el</u> **bebé** (the baby boy) and <u>la</u> **bebé** (the baby girl).

For the people words that end in –R, the feminine form ends in –RA. For example, a male professor is **profesor** / p'ddoh-feh-SOH*RR*, and a female professor is **profesora** / p'ddoh-feh-SOHddah. A male doctor is **doctor** / thohk-<u>T</u>OH*RR*, while a female doctor is **doctora** / thohk-<u>T</u>OHDDah. The plurals are **profesores** / **profesoras** and **doctores** / **doctoras**.

There are some job titles in which both the masculine and the feminine form end in –A. One example is **colega** / coh-LEH-gah (co-worker, male or female). As in the case of the people words that end in –E, only the article ("a" or "the") changes to show male versus female with a job title ending in -A. So, you would say <u>un</u> **colega** for "a male co-worker," but <u>una</u> **colega** for "a female co-worker." The plural is **colegas** (co-workers, colleagues).

You may use the titles **señor** (Mr., gentleman, man), **señora** (Mrs., Ma'am, lady, woman), and **señorita** (Miss, young lady, woman) to talk about others as well as address them directly. For example, you could refer to "the lady from the computer class" as **la señora de la clase de computadoras**.

Finally, you don't usually use **un** or **una** when you give a job title. For example, to say "I'm (a) student," you say **Soy (–) estudiante**. You would only say **un** or **una** to talk about what a unique or special student you are, as in **Soy un (una) estudiante excelente** / ehk-seh-LEHN-<u>t</u>eh (I'm an excellent student).

B) SPECIALTY PEOPLE WORDS (optional)

Refer to, or make up, a list of additional <u>people</u> words that are essential for communication in your specialty area. You may ask your teacher or visit **www.spanishthatworks.org** for ideas.

If you use a dictionary, make sure each word is a noun (person, place or thing) and note the noun's gender (**m.** or **f.**). Look up the word on the Spanish side of the dictionary to double-check the translation or the gender.

Make up a pronunciation guide for your specialty words, using the chart at the beginning of Unit One. Then fill out this blank chart with the twelve most important specialty words. Some may overlap with the basic words. You may also wish to use or make up specialty word flashcards.

SPANISH	PRONUNCIATION	ENGLISH

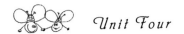

Check for Understanding

People Words. 1) Practice the "Family" words and any specialty "People" words, using study lists or flashcards, until you are familiar with them. Follow the steps outlined in "How to Practice Vocabulary" in Lesson Two.

2) Translate these sentences, using the "Family" words and the examples from Lesson Eight. Answers are in the supplemental section.

1) Your mom needs a book.

2) The boy wants a pencil.

3) The students want more.

4) My parents need help.

5) My dad doesn't need "nothing."

6) The girl student wants a pen.

7) The boy student needs paper.

8) It's not my boyfriend; it's my friend (male).

3) The social titles **señor** (Sir, Mr., man), **señora** (Ma'am, Mrs., lady) and **señorita** (Miss, young lady) are sometimes used with a job title, or in place of a job title. For example, the "director" (**director** / thee-ddek-<u>TOH</u>RR) might be referred to as **el señor director**. A Spanish speaker might say **la señorita de la tienda** (the young lady from the shop) to talk about a store employee. You may wish to review the social titles in Lesson Two.

Lesson Eight Expressions

Yo no.	yoh NOH	I don't, Not me
Bueno, pues...	BWEH-noh pwehss	All right, then...
Está bien.	eh-S<u>T</u>AH b'YEHN	That's fine (okay).
¡Vamos!	BAH-mohss!	Let's go! / We're going!
a	ah	to
a la	ah lah	to the place (f.)
al	ahl	to the place (m.) contraction of **a + el**
hablar	ah-BLAH*RR*	to speak
ahora	ah-OHddah	now
ahorita	ah-oh-DDEE-<u>t</u>ah	right now

Speaking Practice

With a partner, practice the Lesson Eight mini-dialogues, using "People," "Things," and "Places" words. Pay attention to masculine and feminine, singular and plural.

1) In dialogue A, be sure to use the correct form of "my" (**mi or mis**). In dialogues A and C, you can say either **necesito** (I need) or **quiero** (I want). Be careful with the pronunciation of **quiero** / k'YEHddoh.

2) In dialogue B, you can say **la sala**, or pick a place that makes sense.

3) In dialogue C, you can add in places and people words from your specialty module. You can use names of people you know or make up names after the social titles **señor, señora,** and **señorita.**

NOTE: The Spanish word **al** / ahl (to the) is a contraction without apostrophe of **a** / ah (to) and **el** / ehl (the-masculine). Spanish **a + el = al.** However, **a + la** (the-feminine) = **a la** / ah lah, as two separate words.

Speaking Activities

1) Pick a dialogue and act it out. Work with a partner, and use props, if possible.

2) Write a dialogue based on the Lesson Eight mini-dialogues, and use ONLY the vocabulary presented in this lesson and previous lessons. Take dialogues from the text and reorganize them in a creative way.

3) Act out your own dialogue with a partner. Use props, if possible.

More Practice

1) Point out family members from a photo album or pretend that people in a magazine are your family and friends. Say **Es mi...** (It's my...) for one person: **Es mi mamá, Es mi hermano,** etc., and **Son mis...** (They're my...) for more than one: **Son mis padres, Son mis amigos,** etc.

2) Practice saying the "Family" words and Lesson Eight expressions aloud. Make flashcards or study lists. Learn the "Family" words and Lesson Eight expressions by heart. Continue to practice the verbs you have learned so far.

3) Learn any essential people words for your specialty area.

4) Visit **www.spanishthatworks.org** for additional suggestions, practice materials, and links to other resources.

el novio
el estudiante
el colega

la novia
la estudiante
la colega

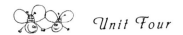

Lesson Eight Mini-Dialogues:
People Words

A) Someone needs something <u>for</u> a family member

1) ¿Qué necesita?	1) What do You need?
2) (Necesito / Quiero) (un / una) <u>item</u> para mi(s) <u>family member(s)</u>.	2) (I need / I want) an <u>item</u> for my <u>family member(s)</u>.
1) Muy bien. Por aquí, por favor.	1) Very well. This way, please.
2) Gracias.	2) Thanks.

FAMILY: familia, papá, mamá, padres, niño, niña, niños, esposo, esposa, hijo, hija, hijos, hermano, hermana, amigo, amiga, amigos, novio, novia

B) Family member needs something

1) Buenas tardes. ¿Necesita ayuda?	1) Good afternoon. Do You need help?
2) Yo no, pero mi <u>family member</u> necesita (un / una / mi / su) <u>item</u>.	2) I don't, but my <u>family member</u> needs (a / my / his or her) <u>item</u>.
1) Y... ¿dónde está su (<u>family member</u>) ahora?	1) And... where is Your (<u>family member</u>) now?
2) Allá, en (la sala / OTHER).	2) Over there, in (the room /OTHER).

FAMILY: papá, mamá, niño, niña, esposo, esposa, hijo, hija, hermano, hermana, amigo, amiga, novio, novia

C) Someone needs to speak with someone else

1) Buenos días. ¿Necesita ayuda?	1) Hello. Do You need help?
2) Bueno, pues... (Necesito / Quiero) hablar con (el /la / mi) _____.	2) Well, so... (I need / I want) to speak with (the / my) _____ (title).
1) Está bien. (Vamos a la oficina. / Vamos al salón de junta. / Vamos a _____.)	1) That's fine. (Let's go to the office. / Let's go to the meeting room. / Let's go to _____).

PEOPLE: profesor, profesora, estudiante (m. & f.), colega (m. & f.), doctor, doctora, señor____, señora____, señorita____, OTHER

EXTRA NOTE:

La familia / lah fah-MEEL-yah (the family)
is the most important social unit in Latino culture.

It is common for several generations of family to
live together in the same household. Adult
children often live at home until they marry.

Some extended family words include:
tío & tía / <u>TEE</u>-oh, <u>TEE</u>-ah (uncle & aunt),
abuelo & abuela / ah-BWEH-loh, ah-BWEH-lah
(grandfather & grandmother)
and **padrino & madrina** / pah-th'DDEE-noh,
mah-th'DDEE-nah (godfather & godmother).

UNIT FIVE:

"I'm a student. I speak a little Spanish."

Lesson 9: I am...

- ❖ State vs. Essence (Estar vs. Ser)
- ❖ Asking Questions with "Está" and "Es"
- ❖ When "I have" is "I am"
- ❖ There is, There are
- ❖ Expressions (Nice to meet you, good, fine, well...)
- ❖ Mini-Dialogues

Lesson 10: How do you say...?

- ❖ Getting What You Want
- ❖ Communication Strategies
- ❖ Expressions (The thing is, a little bit, slower...)
- ❖ More Expressions (U.S., co-worker, blue...)
- ❖ Mini-Dialogues

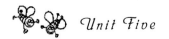

LESSON NINE: I am...
Basic Structures

A) STATE VS. ESSENCE

Much of the challenge of beginning Spanish is to learn the different ways of saying **am**, **is**, and **are**.

In English, we use **I am**, **you are**, **s/he is**, and **they are** to express various states of being of people and objects, including their **location** (where they are), their **state or condition** (how they are), and the "essence" of their **identity** (who or what they are, including name, profession or purpose, and other "essential," or **defining**, characteristics).

Spanish however, makes a distinction between being in a **STATE** (location or condition), and being in **ESSENCE** (name, and "essential" or defining properties). Spanish also uses the verb **HAVE** (**tengo, tiene, tienen**) in certain cases in which English would use "am," "is," "are." For example, in Spanish you say "I have hunger," instead of "I am hungry."

This lesson gives some guidelines to the different ways to say **am**, **is**, and **are**. These guidelines will help you to understand the mini-dialogues.

Look at this Spanish verb:

estoy	eh-S<u>T</u>OY	I am STATE (location, condition)
está	eh-S<u>T</u>AH	You, s/he, it is STATE (location, condition)
están	eh-S<u>T</u>AHN	You all/they are STATE (location, condition)

Estoy, está, están indicate a STATE of being (location, feeling, condition, appearance). Remember: eSTÁ = STAte.

You will use **estoy, está, están** to talk about <u>where</u> people and things are ("in class, at the meeting"), <u>how</u> people are <u>**feeling**</u> ("fine") and to describe the <u>**condition**</u> of things ("busy").

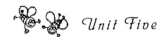

Examples:

¿Dónde está el baño?	Where is the bathroom?
Los estudiantes están en clase.	The students are in class.
Lo siento, no está.	I'm sorry, s/he is not in.
Estoy bien, gracias.	I'm fine, thanks.
Está bien.	It's fine.
El baño está ocupado.*	The bathroom is occupied (busy).

*Be sure to pronounce the "d" in **ocupado** / oh-coo-PAH-thoh as the "th" of "brother."

Now look at this Spanish verb:

soy	soy	I am ESSENCE (definition, name)
es	ehss	You s/he/it is ESSENCE (definition, name)
son	sohn	You all/ they are ESSENCE (definition, name)

Soy, es, son point to the ESSENCE of one's identity, or those ESSENTIAL characteristics which __name__ or __define__ someone or something. You use **soy, es, son** to tell who or what someone or something __is__ (name or definition), what a person or thing __is like__ (the personality), to say when an event __is happening__ or to express __the time__. Remember: ES-SON = ES-SENce (naming, definition). Also remember: "Time is of the essence."

You will use **soy, es, son** to talk about how things **really are,** as opposed to how they look, feel, or where they've been moved to. You will use **soy** to give your name and job, and **es** or **son** to define or name things, to talk about when activities and events are happening, and to give the date and time.

Examples:

Soy Ana. Soy estudiante.*	I'm Ana. I'm (a) student.
¿Qué es? ¿Qué son?	What is it? What are they?
Es un lápiz	It's a pencil.
Es mi hija.	It's my daughter.
La clase es ahora.	The class is now.
La clase es buena.	The class is good.

*You do not say **un / una** when you express your job title, unless you mean "one."

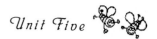

Check for Understanding

State or Essence? Say whether these sentences express STATE (**estoy, está, están**), or ESSENCE (**soy, es, son**). Then translate to Spanish. Answers and explanations are in the supplemental section.

1) Hi, I'm Claudia.

2) The meeting is now.

3) Where is Pedro?

4) "The" Mr. Padilla is busy (ocupado).

5) Is (it) Your child?

6) The paper is for the office.

7) How are You?

8) It's fine. (It's okay.)

9) "The" Mrs. Smith is not in.

10) I am a student.

STATE VS. ESSENCE: Notes

Sometimes "state" vs. "essence" depends on the situation. For example, **is** someone a happy person (definition, identity) or just **feeling** happy today (condition, state of mind)? Sometimes the preference between "state" or "essence" depends on the perspective or dialect of the speaker. For example, **is** the object pretty (definition), or does it **look** pretty (condition)?

Other times, there are clear-cut rules for which verb to use. For example, you <u>always</u> use **soy** to give your job title (**Soy estudiante**), because one's profession is an essential characteristic. You always use **está** when you want to say something is "fine" (**Está bien**), because "fine" is a condition.

In order to use "am," "is," and "are" in conversation, it's helpful to practice complete phrases such as "I'm Margaret" (**Soy Margarita**) and "How are you?" (¿**Cómo está?**), instead of trying to learn the rules for each situation.

Once you know the example, the rule will follow.

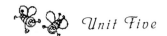

B) ASKING QUESTIONS WITH "ESTÁ" & "ES"

Notice how some of these questions ask about STATE (location or condition), while others ask about ESSENCE (name or definition).

¿Dónde?	THOHN-theh	Where?
¿Dónde está?	THOHN-theh-eh-S<u>T</u>AH?	Where is s/he, it? Where are You?
¿Cómo?	KOH-moh	How?
¿Cómo está?	KOH-moh-eh-S<u>T</u>AH?	How are You? How is s/he, it?

¿Qué?	KEH?	What?
¿Qué es?	kay-EHSS?	What is it? (definition)
¿Quién?	k'YEHN	Who?
¿Quién es?	k'yehnn-EHSS?	Who is it?
¿Cuándo?	KWAHN-thoh	When?
¿Cuándo es?	KWAHN-thoh-EHSS?	When is it?
¿Cuál?	KWAHL?	Which?
¿Cuál es...?	KWAHL-ehss	What is...? (personal data)
¿Cuál es su nombre?	kwah-LEHssoo NOHM-b'ddeh?	What is Your name?

C) WHEN "I HAVE" IS "I AM"

Look at these sentences:

Tengo frío.	TEHNG-goh f'DDEE-oh	I'm cold. (I have cold.)
¿Tiene hambre?	<u>T</u>YEH-neh AHM-b'ddeh	Are You hungry? (Do You have hunger?)

As you can see, Spanish expresses some states of being with **have** or **has** instead of "am," "is," and "are." Since you have a <u>thing</u>, the words used with **tengo, tiene, tienen** are <u>nouns</u>, just like book or pencil.

Other things you "have" rather than "are" include: heat (**calor** / cah-LOH*RR*), thirst (**sed** / SETH), sleepiness (**sueño** / SWEN-yoh), luck (**suerte** / SWAI*RR*-<u>t</u>eh), **fear** (miedo / m'YEH-thoh) and hurriedness (**prisa** / p'DDEE-sah). See the supplemental section for more information.

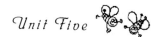

D) THERE IS, THERE ARE

To talk about the general existence of something, use the verb **hay** / AYE.

Look at these sentences:

Hay clase mañana.	aye CLAH-seh mahn-YAH-nah	There is class tomorrow.
Hay dos libros.	aye thoss LEE-b'ddohss	There are two books.
No hay papel.	noh-AYE pah-PEHL	There isn't (any) paper.
¿Hay teléfono?	aye <u>t</u>eh-LEH-foh-noh?	Is there a phone?
No hay problema.	noh-aye-p'ddoh-BLEH-mah	There's no problem.

Hay / aye is an easy verb to use because you use the same form whether you are talking about something singular or plural. Use **hay** / aye when the English translation would be "there is" or "there are." Be careful with pronunciation. The "h" is silent, and "ay" is like the English words "I" or "eye."

Lesson Nine Expressions

Mucho gusto.	MOO-choh GOO-stoh	Much pleasure (to meet you).
El gusto es mío.	ehl GOO-stoh ehs MEE-oh	The pleasure is mine.
bueno	BWEH-noh	good, nice
bien	b'YEHN	well, fine
Muy bien	mooy b'YEHN	Very well
¡Qué bueno!	KEH BWEH-noh!	Great! How nice!
¡Yo también!	yoh <u>t</u>ahm-b'YEHN	Me too!
profesión (f.)	p'ddoh-feh-s'YOHN	profession
Bien, gracias	b'YEHN, g'DAH-s'yahs	Fine (well), thanks
ahora	ah-OHddah	now
Hasta luego.	AH-s<u>t</u>ah LWEH-goh	See you later.
Adiós.	ah-th'YOHSS	Good-bye.

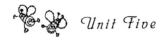

Speaking Practice

Practice the Lesson Nine mini-dialogues. Work with a partner, if possible.

1) Use the dialogues to interview various people. In dialogues A and B, you role play how to introduce yourself and ask questions of a stranger. You may combine or modify the dialogues to make the conversation flow better.
2) You may use your own profession for dialogue B, or just be a student of Spanish.
3) In dialogues C & D, you are using the polite "You" (**usted**) instead of the buddy-buddy "you" (**tú**), so you won't put an –S on **¿Cómo está?** or **¿Dónde está?** This will help you to use the correct form with adults who are not your family or intimate friends.

NOTE: **¿Cómo está?** is the polite way to inquire about the well-being of someone. Unlike the casual "How are you?" in English, which can be used as a greeting, **¿Cómo está?** implies that you know the person and care about the response. To greet someone formally, you would say **Buenos días / Buenas tardes.**

Speaking Activities

1) Pick a dialogue and act it out. Work with a partner, and use props, if possible.
2) Write your own dialogue based on the Lesson Nine mini-dialogues and use ONLY the vocabulary presented in this lesson and previous lessons.
3) Act out your own dialogue. Work with a partner, and use props, if possible.

More Practice

1) Practice saying the Lesson Nine structures and expressions aloud using the pronunciation guide. Work with a partner, if possible.
2) Learn the Lesson Nine structures and expressions by heart. Continue to practice other verbs you have learned. Review any specialty words.
3) Visit **www.spanishthatworks.org** for additional suggestions, practice materials, and links to other resources.

 Lesson Nine Mini-Dialogues:
I am...

A) Meeting people

1) Hola, soy _____. *(Say your name)*	1) Hi, I'm _____. *(Say your name)*
2) Mucho gusto. Soy _____. *(Say your name)*	2) Much pleasure (to meet you). I'm _____. *(Say your name)*
1) El gusto es mío.	1) The pleasure is mine.

B) Asking name and profession

1) ¿Cuál es su nombre?	1) What is Your name?
2) _____. *(Give your name)*	2) _____. *(Give your name)*
1) ¿Y su profesión?	1) And Your profession?
2) Soy (estudiante de español / OTHER).	2) I'm a (Spanish student / OTHER).
1) ¡Qué bueno! (¡Yo también!)	1) How nice! (Me too!)

C) Asking about someone's well-being

1) ¡Hola! ¿Cómo está?	1) Hi! How are You feeling?
2) Muy bien, gracias. ¿Y usted?	2) Very well, thanks. And You?
1) Bien, gracias.	1) Fine, thanks.

D) On the cell phone with someone you know

1) *Phone rings.* (¿Aló? /¿Bueno?)	1) *Phone rings.* (Hello? /Hello?-Mex.)
2) ¡Hola! Soy _____. ¿Dónde está?	2) Hi! It's _____. Where are You?
1) En la clase de español.	1) In Spanish class.
2) ¿Cuándo es la clase?	2) When is the class?
1) Ahora.	1) Now.
2) Ah, perdón. Hasta luego.	2) Oh, sorry. See You later.
1) Está bien. Adiós, hasta luego.	1) That's fine. Bye, see You later.

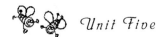

EXTRA NOTE:

A useful expression for asking someone you know
how things are going is **¿Qué tal?** / keh <u>T</u>AHL?

It can be used similarly to **¿Cómo está?**
to inquire about someone's well-being:
¡Hola! ¿Qué tal? (Hi! How's it going?)

¿Qué tal? can also be used to ask how something
else is or has been, without having to use a verb:

¿Qué tal el trabajo? (How is the job?)
¿Qué tal la clase? (How was the class?)

For other handy phrases, see the
"Social Expressions and Basic Customer Service"
portion of the supplemental section.

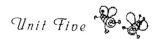

LESSON TEN: How do you say...?

Basic Structures

A) GETTING WHAT YOU WANT

For everything that you want to accomplish by using language, there are many ways to get the job done. For example, if you want to use the telephone, you can say, "I want to use the phone," but you can also say "Is there a phone?" "Do you have a phone?" "Where is the phone?" "I'd like to use the phone," "I need to make a call," "Phone, please," "Will you give me the phone?" or just "May I?"

When you are starting out learning a language, it is helpful to think of the **function** of what you are doing with the language, rather than on the translation of what you would want to say in English.

One reason for this is that when you are first learning a language, you do not know all of the vocabulary and grammar necessary to translate from your native language. Another, and perhaps more important reason, is that Spanish is not a word-for-word translation from English, so a direct translation will not always be appropriate.

One of the most basic functions of language is getting what you want from your environment. You learned an easy way to do this in Lesson Two, with the simple construction "<u>Item</u>, please." See if you can recall some of the other ways you have learned to ask for what you want. (NOTE: In Unit Six you will learn how to say what you want <u>to do</u>, and how to ask others to do things.)

Check for Understanding

Phone, please.   Translate into Spanish. NOTE: **¿Me da?** / meh-THAH (Will you give me?) can be used in the same way that "Can I have?" is used in English.

1) I want the phone, please.

2) Do You have a phone?

3) Where is the phone?

4) Is there a phone?

5) Will You give me the phone?

6) The telephone, please.

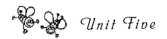

B) COMMUNICATION STRATEGIES

Up until now, you have been acquiring some basic tools to communicate with others about people, places and things. But what do you do when people don't say things the way you practiced them? Here are some possible "what if" scenarios:

What if someone speaks too quickly? What if someone uses an unfamiliar word? What if you think you know what someone is talking about, but you're not sure? What if you can't remember a word? What if there is a complete breakdown in communication and you don't know what to do?

Fortunately, there are strategies and expressions that can help you to better communicate with people, using the Spanish you already know. Let's deal with these "what if's" one at a time.

What if someone speaks too quickly?

To a person who is not fluent in a language, it often seems as if the speakers of the language talk very quickly. Here are some expressions that can help.

¿Cómo?	COH-moh?	Pardon me? (when you don't hear or understand)
No entiendo.	noh-ehn-t'YEHN-thoh	I don't understand.
Repita.	rreh-PEE-tah	Repeat (polite form).
Más despacio.	mahss theh-SPAH-s'yoh	More slowly.

It can also help to let the person know you are not completely fluent in Spanish.

Perdón	pairr-THOHN	Excuse me, sorry
Disculpe	thee-SKOOL-peh	Excuse me, sorry
Lo siento	loh s'YEHN-toh	I'm sorry
No hablo mucho español.	noh-AH-bloh MOO-choh eh-spahn-YOHL	I don't speak much Spanish.
Hablo sólo un poco de español.	AH-bloh SOH-loh oon POH-coh theh eh-spahn-YOHL	I speak only a little Spanish.

What if someone uses an unfamiliar word?

Sometimes you may understand the gist of what someone says, but not understand the specific thing that he or she is talking about. In this case, try to single out the word or words that you don't understand. Then try these expressions.

No entiendo <u>X</u>.	noh-ehn-<u>T</u>YEHN-thoh …	I don't understand <u>X</u>.
¿Qué es <u>X</u>?	KAY-ehss…?	What is <u>X</u>?

If that fails, try this.

Escriba aquí, (por favor).	eh-sk'DEE-ba-ah-KEE…	Write here, (please).

Having others write things down can be a good strategy. Often you will recognize a word in its written form that you could not understand in speech. For example, the word "hay-oh-loh-HEE-ah" doesn't seem like English at all, until you see it spelled: **geología**. Then it's easy to guess that it means "geology."

What if you think you know what someone is talking about, but you're not sure?

Sometimes you may think you know what someone needs, but you're not sure. In this case, you should confirm your hunch about what you think the person is saying. If possible, ask the person a yes / no question. It doesn't even have to be a complete sentence—often one word will do.

For example, if you think a person is looking for the restroom, you can say **¿Baño?** / BAHN-yoh? (Bathroom?) as a question and then wait to see if you guessed correctly. You would ask for clarification if an English speaker said something you didn't quite understand, too.

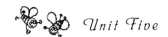

Or, let's say someone is talking about a **novela** / noh-VEH-lah **en español**. You think it means "novel in Spanish," but you're not sure. In this case, you can confirm your hunch with one of these expressions.

Novela... es un libro, ¿no?   Novela... it's a book, right?

Novela... es un libro, ¿verdad?   Novela... it's a book, right?

...¿no?	NOH?	...right?, don't you?
...¿verdad?	bai*rr*-THAH-th	...right?

The person might answer **Sí**, or **No**, since the word **novela** is used for books of fiction, comic books, and even television soap operas. The important thing is that you are communicating. You would do this sort of question and answer process if an English speaker asked you about something unfamiliar.

Let's say someone is talking about a **película** / peh-LEE-coo-lah. It doesn't sound like anything in English, but the context makes you think that it's something you look at. So, you might ask...

¿Qué es? ¿Un libro? ¿Un video?   What is it? A book? A video?

The answer might be, **Es un video** / bee-THEY-oh, since **película** means "movie."

Of course, if you truly do not understand, you can always say **No entiendo** / noh ehn-T̲YEHN-thoh (I don't understand), or **No hablo español** (I don't speak Spanish). Then you can say **Un momento** / oon moh-MEHN-t̲oh and go get someone who can help. But don't give up too soon! Most of the time you can figure out what someone needs with very few words.

What if you can't remember a word?

It's common when learning another language to know that you know what to say, but to not be able to recall the words. In this case, you need to let the speaker know that you have heard the question, and that you are considering your answer. Often you just need more time!

The following expressions are helpful when you need more time.

Bueno...	BWEH-noh	Well, all right, good
Pues...	PWEHss	Well...so...then
Mire...	MEEddeh	See...
Sabe...	SAH-beh	You know...
Es que...	EHSS-keh	(the thing) is that...
Este...	EHSS-<u>t</u>eh	"um," "like"
...o sea...	oh-SAY-ah	I mean, "like," "um"
...y... or ...e...	EEEEE / EHHHH	"ummmmm"
Un momento.	oon moh-MEHN-<u>t</u>oh	One moment

Native Spanish speakers use filler and clarification expressions such as these all the time, so knowing a few will also help you to understand what people are telling you.

Also, when dealing with others in person, make full use of body language and visual cues. You can point, hold up examples of what you are talking about, and mime actions such as writing or eating. You do have to be careful with gestures, because some gestures do not have equivalents in other languages, and can even cause insult. However, things like pointing out what you want should not cause any misunderstanding.

Native speakers will generally be supportive of your efforts to speak Spanish, so don't feel that you have to say everything perfectly.

These expressions are helpful when you don't know a word.

eso	EHSSoh	"that" (point to item)
esto	EHSS-<u>t</u>oh	"this" (point to item)
Es como (un / una)....	ehss COH-moh	It's similar to a...
por ejemplo	POHddeh HEM-ploh	for example
¿Cómo se dice... (en inglés / español)?	KOH-moh say THEE-say	How does one say... (in English / Spanish)?
En inglés, es <u>X</u>.	ehn-een-GLEHSS, ehs...	In English, it's <u>X</u>.

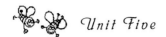

What if there is a complete breakdown in communication?

Occasionally you might feel like you're in over your head and you need some help. The first thing to do is to determine if the person (or someone with the person) knows any English. It is possible that the person understands much more than he or she can speak, just like you.

Even if the person speaks or understands very little spoken English, it may be that he or she knows how to read it. So if you do turn to English, pronounce each syllable distinctly, as if you were reading. For example, instead of "wahddahya gonna do?" you might need to say "What—are—you—going—to—do?"

These expressions will come in handy.

¿Entiende inglés?	ehn-t'YEHN-theh een-GLEHSS?	Do You, s/he understand English?
¿Habla inglés?	AH-blah een-GLEHSS?	Do You, s/he speak English?
Sólo ...un poco	SOH-loh ...oon POH-koh	Only ...a little bit
...un poquito	...oon poh-KEE-toh	...a little tiny bit

Most Spanish speakers will appreciate that you are making an effort, so don't worry about not being completely fluent in the language. However, if a situation does arise in which you need help (either from another person or from your dictionary), these expressions will be useful.

No sé.	noh-SEH	I don't know.
No entiendo.	noh-ehn-t'YEHN-thoh	I don't understand.
Un momento	oon moh-MEHN-toh	One moment
No hay problema	noh-"AYE" p'ddoh-BLEH-mah	No problem, it's not a problem
Mi colega (amigo, hijo, etc.) habla muy bien.	mee coh-LEH-gah (etc.) AH-blah mooy b'YEHN	My co-worker (friend, child, etc.) speaks very well.

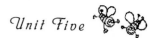
Lesson Ten Expressions

si (no accent mark)	see	if
le doy	leh THOY	I give You ("to You I give")
celular (m.)	seh-loo-LAH*RR*	cell phone
Los Estados Unidos	lohss eh-S̲TAH-thohss oo-NEE-thohss	The United States
ya	yah	already
colega (m. or f.)	coh-LEH-gah	co-worker (m. or f.)
Es todo.	ehss T̲OH-thoh	That's all.
azul	ah-SOOL	blue

OTHER: Pick the expressions from this lesson that you think will be most helpful for you to know and learn those first.

For more information on social expressions, see the "Social Language" portion of the supplemental section, starting on page S-11. You can also visit **www.spanishthatworks.org** for a handy reference sheet.

And remember, it can take years to become completely fluent in another language, but it only takes a few seconds to smile.

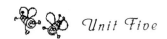

Speaking Practice

Practice the Lesson Ten mini-dialogues. Go through each dialogue four or five times. Work with a partner if possible.

1) Many Spanish speakers use "filler" words such as **bueno, pues, sabe, y..., o sea** and **es que** when they speak. Dialogue A gives you an idea of what you may need to mentally "weed out" in order to understand someone.

2) In dialogue A, the partner playing the part of the Spanish speaker will first ask about an <u>item</u> and then later ask about the <u>item(s)</u>. (You can keep the item in the singular if it makes more sense.) This dialogue helps you practice **un / una, los / las**, and the plural –S or –ES endings. Use your "Things" words.

3) In dialogue B, partner #1 can try to imitate a native speaker talking quickly.

4) In dialogue C, you can quiz each other about how to say various words, using your list or flashcards. You can use dialogue C to review vocabulary.

5) In dialogue D, either partner can be the Spanish or the English speaker. The Spanish speaker may talk about a <u>child</u> that speaks well, and the English speaker may talk about a <u>co-worker</u> or <u>friend</u> who speaks well.

6) In dialogues E and F, use the examples given and then improvise with vocabulary words that you know.

Speaking Activities

1) Pick a dialogue and act it out. Work with a partner, and use props, if possible.

2) Write your own dialogue based on the Lesson Ten mini-dialogues, and use ONLY the vocabulary presented in this lesson and previous lessons.

3) Act out your own dialogue. Work with a partner, and use props, if possible.

More Practice

1) Practice saying the Lesson Ten expressions aloud, using the pronunciation guide. Work with a partner if possible. Review the various ways of getting what you want.

2) Review the communication strategies, and learn by heart the expressions that you like best and that you think will be the most useful.

3) Practice your verbs, using flashcards or study lists, until you know them without having to think. This will build fluency and prepare you for Unit Six.

4) Visit **www.spanishthatworks.org** for additional suggestions, practice materials, and links to other resources.

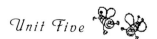
 Lesson Ten Mini-Dialogues:
How do you say...?

A) Someone speaks quickly and uses filler words

1) Bueno pues, sabe, es que, quiero (un / una) <u>item</u>, ¿no? Pero no sé dónde está eso, y..., pues, o sea, no hablo mucho inglés.	1) Well, you know, the thing is, I want an <u>item</u>, right? But I don't know where that is, and..., um... like, I don't speak much English.
2) ¿Cómo? Repita, por favor. No hablo mucho español.	2) Pardon me? Repeat, please. I don't speak much Spanish.
1) Ah, perdón. ¿Dónde está(n) (los / las) <u>item(s)</u>?	1) Oh, sorry. Where is (are) the <u>item(s)</u>?

B) Person asks you something and you don't understand

1) *(Quickly)* ¿Está bien si le doy el número de teléfono de mi (casa / trabajo / oficina / celular) en los Estados Unidos?	1) *(Quickly)* Is it okay if I give You the telephone number of my (house / job / office / cell) in the United States?
2) ¿Cómo? No entiendo. Más despacio, por favor.	2) Pardon me? I don't understand. Slower, please.
1) *(Faster)* Pues... ¿Le doy el número de teléfono de mi (casa / trabajo / oficina / celular) en los Estados Unidos?	1) *(Faster)* Well... Shall I give You the telephone number of my (house / job / office / cell) in the United States?
2) (Escriba aquí, por favor. / Un momento. Mi colega habla español.)	2) (Write here, please. / One moment. My co-worker speaks Spanish.)

C) Learning new words

1) ¿Cómo se dice ____ en (español / inglés)?	1) How does one say _____ in (Spanish / English)?
2) _____.	2) _____.

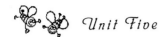

D) Negotiating communication

1) ¿(Habla/ Entiende) Ud. (español / inglés)?	1) Do You (speak / understand) (Spanish / English)?
2) Sólo un (poco / poquito).	2) Only a (little bit / tiny little bit).
1) Es que no (hablo / entiendo) mucho (inglés/ español).	1) The thing is, I don't (speak / understand) much (English / Spanish).
2) No hay problema. Mi (hijo(a) / colega / amigo(a)) habla muy bien. Un momento.	2) No problem. My (child / co-worker / friend) speaks very well. One moment.

E) Trying to explain yourself

1) Quiero (una pluma / OTHER item), por favor.	1) I want (a pen / OTHER item), please.
2) ¿Cómo? No entiendo. ¿Qué es "una pluma" / "OTHER") ?	2) Pardon me? I don't understand. What is "a pen" / "OTHER") ?
1) Es como un (lápiz / OTHER), pero azul.	1) It's like a (pencil /OTHER), but blue.
2) Ah, ya entiendo. ¿Algo más?	2) Oh, I understand already. Anything else?
1) No. *(Pause.)* Es todo. Gracias.	1) No. *(Pause.)* That's all. Thanks.

F) Confirming what you understood

1) Quiero (un celular /eso / OTHER), por favor. *Points.*	1) I want (a cell phone / "that" / OTHER), please. *Points.*
2) Es (un teléfono / esto / OTHER), ¿no?	2) It's (a phone / "this" / OTHER), right?
1) Sí. Eso es.	1) Yes, that's it.

EXTRA NOTE:

In Spanish, a double negative such as
"I don't understand nothing" is not only
acceptable grammar—it is required!

When a sentence starts with **no** (don't), the other
words in the sentence will be negative, too.
So, "I don't understand anything," is
No entiendo nada / NAH-thah (nothing).

Also, remember that **no** by itself just means **no**.
To mean **no** (and not **don't**), you must pause.
So, "No. I understand a lot," is
No. (Pause). **Entiendo mucho** / MOO-choh.

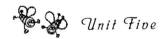

UNIT SIX:

"Do you want to speak in Spanish?"

Lesson 11: Actions

- ❖ Basic Actions
- ❖ Specialty Actions
- ❖ Making Requests with Infinitives
- ❖ Other "To Action" Expressions
- ❖ Using Infinitives to Describe Intent
- ❖ Expressions (Thanks for your help...)
- ❖ Mini-Dialogues

Lesson 12: I want to read!

- ❖ Two Verbs Together (Want / need + actions)
- ❖ One Special Case (Have vs. have to)
- ❖ New Verbs (Can, let's go, go)
- ❖ Expressions (You can do that...)
- ❖ Mini-Dialogues

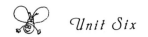

LESSON ELEVEN: Actions

A) BASIC ACTIONS-Core vocabulary

beber	beh-BAI*RR*	to drink
comer	coh-MAI*RR*	to eat
escribir	eh-sk'dee-BEE*RR*	to write
hablar	ah-BLAH*RR*	to speak, talk
hacer	ah-SAI*RR*	to do, to make
ir	EE*RR* (close to "Eater")	to go
leer	leh-AI*RR* (lay-AI*RR*)	to read
mirar	mee-ddAH*RR*	to look, watch
poner	poh-NAI*RR*	to put
regresar	*rr* eh-g'deh-SAH*RR*	to return
tomar	<u>t</u>oh-MAH*RR*	to take (also to drink)
usar	oo-SAH*RR*	to use

The "Basic Actions" words are **infinitives**, or verbs that do not show <u>who</u> is doing an action. In English, the infinitive is often expressed as "to, plus a verb." For example, "to read," "to take," and "to return" indicate general actions, or the idea of the action. They don't say someone is doing the action.

Spanish infinitives end in –R (either –AR, -ER, or –IR). This is the "raw" form of the verb, and is what you would find if you looked in a dictionary. You need to pronounce the final –R (as the "dder" in "ladder" if you can't say the trill yet) so that a Spanish speaker knows you are saying "to, plus a verb."

Sometimes the pronoun **se** / seh, which you may think of as meaning "self," is attached to the –R. Often the **se** conveys a meaning of doing something to or for one<u>self</u>. For example, the verb **mirar** means "to look at," while **mirar<u>se</u>** can mean "to look at oneself," or "to seem."

Verbs that end in -RSE change to –RME when you say "to myself" or "to me." For example, **mirarse** means "to look at <u>oneself</u>" and **mirar<u>me</u>** means "to look at me or <u>myself</u>." **Ponerse** means "to put something on <u>oneself</u>," and **poner<u>me</u>** means "to put something on <u>me</u> or <u>myself</u>."

B) SPECIALTY ACTIONS (optional)

Refer to, or make up, a list of additional <u>actions</u> words (infinitive verbs ending in –R or -RSE), that are essential for communication in your specialty area. You may ask your teacher or visit **www.spanishthatworks.org** for ideas.

If you use a dictionary, make sure the word is a verb (action word). In the dictionary, verbs are indicated with a **v.** (verb, verbo). There may be other letters after the **v.**, such as **v. irr.** (verbo irregular). To double-check the translation, look up the verb on the Spanish side of the dictionary.

Make up a pronunciation guide for your specialty verbs, using the "Saying & Understanding" chart at the beginning of Unit One. Then fill out this blank chart with the twelve most important specialty words. Some may overlap with the basic words. You may also wish to use or make up specialty word flashcards.

SPANISH	PRONUNCIATION	ENGLISH

Note about pronouns

As with the pronoun **se** / seh (-self), pronouns such as **me** / meh (to me, me), **le** / leh (to him, her, You), **lo** / loh (him, it), and **la** /lah (her, it) may be added directly to the end of an infinitive. For example, **hablar<u>le</u>** means "to talk to him, her, or You," and **leer<u>lo</u>** means "to read it."

You will not be actively practicing many pronouns in this course, so for now, just practice the examples that are given.

Check for Understanding

Actions & More Actions. Practice saying the "Actions" words, both basic and specialty, until you are familiar with them. Follow the three steps in "How to Practice Vocabulary" outlined in Lesson Two.

As you learn the words, pay close attention when the <u>English translation</u> includes an extra word such as "at," "to," or "for." These words are included in the Spanish infinitive, so you should learn them together.

For example, **escuchar** (eh-skoo-CHAHRR) means "to listen <u>to</u>." Therefore, "to listen <u>to</u> music" would be simply **escuchar música**. The "to" is already included in the verb, so you don't need to add it. With the verb **llevar** / yeh-VAHRR ("to carry or take along"), on the other hand, you will need to add the word **a** / AH (to), when you talk about carrying something "to" somewhere, because the "to" is <u>not</u> automatically included in the verb. If you learn the English translations for the verbs <u>exactly</u> as they are given, it will be easier to keep things straight later on.

Also pay attention to whether the infinitive ends in –AR, -ER, or –IR (with or without the pronoun **se**) and learn the verb correctly. This information will be important to you later on, should you decide to study more Spanish.

Pick the "Actions" words you know you will need for your own particular situation and learn those first, using the steps outlined in Lesson Two. Later, you can use a dictionary to learn infinitive verbs that are not on your list. For tips on how to learn new vocabulary, refer to the supplemental section, pages S-6 to S-9.

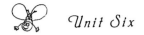

C) MAKING REQUESTS WITH INFINITIVES

Spanish direct commands such as "Look!" "Don't do that!" and "I want you to listen!" require knowledge of verb conjugations beyond the scope of this practical course. However, you can easily make formal requests by using the following "formula" expressions and an infinitive verb.

PLEASE / PLEASE DON'T

Favor de... + infinitive	fah-VOHRR theh	Please <u>action</u>
Favor de no... + inf.	fah-VOHRR theh NOH	Please don't <u>action</u>

Favor de escribir su nombre.   Please write Your name.
Favor de no comer aquí.   Please don't eat here.

NOTE: "Please" all by itself is **por favor**. However, you drop the "por" when you give a command with an infinitive.

Check for Understanding

Please Do & Don't. Using your "Actions" words, come up with some examples of what you would like people to **Please do,** and **Please don't.**

See the answer key in the supplemental section for examples.

Favor de…	Favor de no…

Requests on written signs

On a written sign, you can use just the infinitive (or NO plus the infinitive).

Poner libros aquí	Put Books Here
No comer ni beber	No Eating or (nor) Drinking

You may include the "please" if you wish:

Favor de poner libros aquí	Please Put Books Here
Favor de no comer ni beber	No Eating (nor) Drinking Please

NOTE: In these "formula" commands, the English translation will sometimes have an –ING ending, as in "No Eating or Drinking" or "No Smoking." However, Spanish still uses the infinitive (-R, -RSE, etc. ending).

D) OTHER "TO ACTION" EXPRESSIONS

IT'S (NOT) ALLOWED

Se permite... + *inf*	say-pai*rr*-MEE-<u>teh</u>	It's permitted (allowed) to <u>action</u>
No se permite... + *inf*	NOH say-pai*rr*-MEE-<u>teh</u>	It's not permitted to <u>action</u>

Se permite escribir con lápiz.	It's allowed to write with pencil.
No se permite hablar.	It's not allowed to talk.

NOTE: The pronoun **se** / seh can translate as "oneself" or "one," so you may also think of **Se permite** as meaning "One is permitted." The **se** is often used when the people doing an action are not named. For example, **Se habla español** means "(Some)one speaks Spanish" or "Spanish is spoken (by unnamed individuals)."

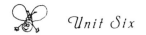

❀❀❀❀❀
Check for Understanding

It's allowed / It's not allowed. You are telling someone what is and is not permitted. List two or three infinitives from the "Actions" words for each expression. See the supplemental section for examples.

Se permite...   **No se permite...**

Other Expressions.   There are many other expressions which may be used with an infinitive, such as **Es hora de… +inf.** (It's time to…), **Me gusta… + inf.** (I like to…), and **Le gusta…+ inf.** (You, s/he like to…). Refer to the supplemental section (p. S-33) for more information.

E) USING INFINITIVES TO DESCRIBE INTENT

In Lesson Three, you learned how to describe things by saying the main noun, a functional word, and then a describing noun.

You can use infinitives like describing nouns, and they don't change ending, even if the English translation has an –ING ending. If you are describing the **intended purpose or use** of an object, you will use **para** (intended for) as the functional word.

papel para escribir	paper for writing
una pluma para escribir	a pen to write (with)

You can use **para + infinitive** to express or ask about an intended action.

¿Es para leer en casa?	Is (this) to read at home?
¿Es para comer ahora?	Is (this) to eat / for eating now?

Lesson Eleven Expressions

A	ah	to (a location)
al (contraction of a + el)*	ahl	to the (m.)
esto	EH-stoh	this (unspecified thing)
eso	EH-soh	that (unspecified thing)
tarde	TAHRR-theh	late (also afternoon)
más tarde	mahss TAHRR-theh	later
afuera	ah-FWEH-ddah	outside
para + *infinitive*	PAH-ddah + (...)	to (do s.t.), in order to (do s.t.), for (doing s.t.)
Gracias por su ayuda.	g'ddAH-s'yahss pohrr soo ah-YOO-thah	Thanks for (receipt of) your help.

*NOTE: Spanish does not use apostrophes. The other contraction in Spanish is **de + el (del)** which means **of the**.

Speaking Practice

Practice the Lesson Eleven mini-dialogues. Use the actions listed at first. Later, you can improvise. The dialogues will show the "Actions" word as <u>to action</u>, so you remember that these are infinitives. In dialogue C, use your "Things" words and pick an intended use that makes sense for the context.

Speaking Activities

1) Pick a dialogue and act it out. Work with a partner, and use props, if possible.
2) Write a dialogue based on the Lesson Eleven mini-dialogues.
3) Act out your own dialogue. Work with a partner, and use props, if possible.

More Practice

1) Practice saying the "Actions" words aloud, using the pronunciation guide. Pay attention to whether the verb ends in –AR, -ER, or –IR (with or without –SE).
2) Choose twelve to fifteen of the most essential "Actions" words, or infinitive verbs, (including any specialty verbs), and learn these by heart first. Then review the remaining "Actions." Use memory devices to learn the new words.
3) Study the structures in sections C) and D). Make flashcards or study lists.
4) Visit **www.spanishthatworks.org** for additional practice materials and links.

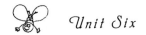

Lesson Eleven Mini-Dialogues:
Actions

A) Asking someone to do / not do something

1) (Señor / Señora / niños), (Favor de / Favor de no) <u>to action</u>.	1) (Sir / Ma'am / children), (Please / Please don't) <u>to action</u>.
2) (Ah, bueno / Ah, perdón).	2) (Oh, okay / Oh, sorry).

ACTIONS: poner eso allá, regresar mañana, hacer eso, leer el libro, beber Coca-cola aquí, hablar, ir a la sala de_____, mirar esto, comer afuera, hacer el trabajo, escribir con pluma, escribir su nombre, OTHER

B) Telling someone if something is permitted...or not

1) Sí, se permite <u>to action</u>.	1) Yes, it's permitted <u>to action</u>.
OR	
1) No, lo siento. No se permite <u>to action</u>.	1) No, I'm sorry. It's not permitted <u>to action</u>.
2) (Gracias por su ayuda / Ah, perdón).	2) (Thanks for Your help / Oh, sorry).

ACTIONS: comer aquí, usar las computadoras, poner eso aquí, ir afuera, regresar mañana, ir más tarde, usar el baño, hacer esto, escribir con lápiz, regresar tarde, hablar aquí, usar el teléfono, beber agua, OTHER

C) Saying what something is and what it's for

1) ¿Qué es esto?	1) What is this?
2) Es (un / una) <u>item</u>. Es para (escribir / tomar / regresar mañana / usar ahora / leer más tarde).	2) It's an <u>item</u>. It's (to write / to take / to return tomorrow / to use now / to read later).
1) Ah bueno, gracias.	1) Oh, okay, thanks.

EXTRA NOTE:

It's very helpful to use memory devices when
you are trying to learn new verbs.

To learn **tomar** / <u>t</u>oh-MAHRR (to take),
for example, you might see yourself saying,
"I'm going **to take** a **tomato**."

The best memory devices are those
which reflect how the word sounds.

So, to learn **leer** / lay-AIRR (to read),
imagine yourself on the beach in Hawaii,
wearing a **lei** and reading in the open **air**, saying
"**Lei air**! It's the best way **to read**!"

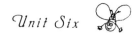

LESSON TWELVE: I want to read!

Basic Structures

A) TWO VERBS TOGETHER

Look at these structures.

Quiero un libro.	I want a book.
Quiero leer.	I want to read.
Quiero leer un libro.	I want to read a book.

¿Necesita mi dirección?	Do You need my address?
¿Necesita escribir?	Do You need to write?
¿Necesita escribir mi dirección?	Do You need to write my address?

Spanish verbs that end in -R (-RSE, etc.) are infinitives, or "to, plus a verb."
You can use infinitives with the verbs you already know ("I have," "You need,"
"You all want," etc.) to make sentences. You can use the infinitive the same way
you would use a noun—after the main verb. Infinitives that end in -R will not
change ending when you use them after another verb.

By using this two-part verb method, you can construct complete sentences
without having to learn how to conjugate (change the ending of) every new verb.

Check for Understanding

Want to / Need to. Translate the following sentences. Do NOT use extra
words for "I" or "they." These words are not required. You <u>may</u> use the words
for "You" and "You all." See the supplemental section for answers.

1) Do You want to write with pen?

4) You don't need to write with pen.

2) I need to read this.

5) My mom needs to use the phone.

3) They want to look at the book.

6) Do You all want to go?

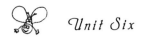

NOTE: You **CANNOT** translate "I want **you**" (to do something) or "I need **you**" (to do something), word for word, directly from English. If you do, it will sound like "I want /love YOU (...);" "I need YOU (...)."

The two-part verb formula only works when it is ONE person wanting or needing to do something. It does **NOT** work for wanting or needing someone else to do something. In Spanish you say, "I want that (**que** / keh) you **do** something," which requires knowledge of verb conjugations and the subjunctive mood.

For now, just use **Favor de...** when you want to make a request of someone else. The fact that you want or need something is implied.

B) ONE SPECIAL CASE: HAVE VS. HAVE TO

Look at these structures.

Tengo un libro.	I have a book.
Tengo que leer un libro.	I have to read a book.

Some verbs take an extra word before an infinitive.

In the case of **tengo, tiene, tienen**, you add the word **que** / KEH (that-what). It doesn't translate into anything that makes sense— you just have to say it. So you will say **tengo que** + infinitive, **tiene que** + infinitive, and **tienen que** + infinitive.

Check for Understanding

Have to. Translate the following sentences. Do NOT use any extra words for "I," "he," or "she." You may use the words for "You" and "You all." Remember to use **que** / KEH before the infinitive. Answers are in the supplemental section.

1) He has to write with pen.

2) Do You have to use the telephone?

3) She doesn't have to return.

4) I have to go to the office.

❀❀❀❀
Sentence Building

To practice making sentences with a two-part verb, it's helpful to use a "sentence builder." Visit **www.spanishthatworks.org** or see the supplemental section (p. S-50) for instructions about how to make your own. Use the sentence builder as follows:

1) Make sentences, going from left to right. Look at the Spanish words and build from there. Don't think of things that you would like to say in English and then look for the words. Just play with it and see what you can create.

2) Work with a partner. Partner #1 makes up a sentence, picking words from the sentence builder. Partner #2 has to translate the sentence. (**NOTE:** The focus of this activity is to practice understanding, not to build "important" sentences. Partner #1 should just pick the first words that come, without paying too much attention to what they mean. That's Partner #2's job.)

3) Make sentences from the sentence builder that you would like to be able to use in conversation. Write them down and check them with someone who has a good command of Spanish.

C) NEW VERBS THAT CAN BE USED IN THE SAME WAY

There are many other verbs that can be used with an infinitive to make a sentence. The following verb is used to talk about things you **are able**, or **permitted** to do.

MAY, CAN

puedo	PWAY-thoh	I can, I may, may I?
puede	PWAY-theh	You, s/he can, may
pueden	PWAY-thehn	You all, they can, may

NOTES: Pronunciation of the "d" as the "th" in "brother" is <u>very</u> important with this verb. If you pronounce it with an English "d," it may sound like an "r" to a Spanish speaker: "puero, puere," which doesn't mean anything.

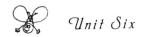
Also, Spanish does NOT make the distinction between something you **can** (are able) and **may** (are permitted) to do. However, it does make a distinction between something you can or can't do because you **are able**, and something you can or can't do because you **know how**.

The verb for "knowing how" is the same as for knowing information: **sé** (I know), **sabe** (You, s/he knows). See the supplemental section for details.

Check for Understanding

Can & May. Translate to Spanish. Do NOT use an extra word for "I." You <u>may</u> use the word for "You." Answers are in the supplemental section.

1) May I read this?

2) You can write with pen.

3) My dad can't write with pencil.

4) I can't go.

"LET'S…"

Vamos a … + <u>place</u>.	BAH-mohss-ah	Let's go / we're going to… <u>place</u>.
Vamos a…+ <u>infinitive</u>.	BAH-mohss-ah	Let's (go) <u>action</u> / We're going to <u>action</u>.

The verb **vamos** / BAH-mohss (we go / let's go) can be used both as a command ("Let's…!") and as a statement about what you will do ("We're going to…"). The difference in meaning is conveyed by your voice.

NOTE: The Spanish preposition **a** /ah means "to" when talking about location. It does NOT mean "at" a location. Also, "b" and "v" are interchangeable in Spanish, so although **BAH-mohss** is more common, you could also say **VAH-mohss**.

Vamos a la oficina.
¡Vamos a la oficina!

We are going to the office.
Let's go to the office!

Vamos a comer.
¡Vamos a comer!

We are going to eat.
Let's eat!

NOTE: The verb ending for "we" is always **–MOS**. You will want to recognize "we" verbs when you hear them, but for now you can get by without having to use them in speech. For example, to express the concept of "we have," you can use an "I" verb (**tengo**), or a "third party" and verb, (**la oficina tiene**), and it will get the job done. However, **vamos** is a good "we" verb to learn because it can be used as a command. For more information about "we" verbs, see the supplemental section.

Check for Understanding

Let's go! Translate to Spanish. Do not use an extra word for "we." It's already included in the verb. Answers are in the supplemental section.

1) Let's read this.

2) Let's use a pen.

3) We're going to the meeting now.

4) Let's go to the office.

I'M GOING, I GO...

Here are some other forms of "go."

Voy a...	BOY-ah	I'm going to
Va a...	BAH-ah	You, s/he is going to
Van a...	BAHNnah	You all, they are going to

Voy, va, van (like **vamos**) can be used to indicate both a place you are going to, and something you are going to do. If you are talking about something you are going **to do**, then you <u>always</u> use **a** / ah (to) plus the infinitive.

Voy a la clase.
Voy a tomar la clase.

I'm going to the class.
I'm going to take the class.

¿Va al patio / PAH-t'yoh?
¿Va a leer en el patio?

Are You going to the patio?
Are You going to read on the patio?

***NOTE:** The contraction (without apostrophe) of **a + el** (**al**) means <u>to the</u>. The other contraction in Spanish is **de + el** (**del**), which means <u>of the</u>.

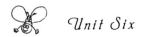

You will usually use **a / ah** after **voy, va, van, vamos**, because you almost always are going "to" somewhere. If you do not say where you are going, you can omit the **a / ah** (to). For example, "I'm not going" is simply **No voy.**

When you use an infinitive with **voy, va, van, vamos**, you <u>must</u> say the **a /ah.** Like **tengo, tiene, tienen + que**, this is a special case in which there is an extra word between the first verb and the infinitive.

Va a pagar.	baah-pah-*GAHRR**	You, s/he is going to pay.
¿Qué va a hacer?	KEH baah-SAI*RR?**	What are You, s/he going to do?

*NOTE: the words **va / BAH** and **a / ah** usually blend together in spoken speech to sound like one long syllable. If the word that follows also starts with an "ah" sound, it joins in the blend.

Check for Understanding

I'm going to. Translate to Spanish. Do NOT use any extra words for "she" or "I." Answers are in the supplemental section.

1) I'm going to read this.

2) Are You going to the class?

3) She's going to the meeting room.

4) You are going to take the class.

D) OTHER VERBS USED IN THE SAME FASHION

With this two-verb method, you can create most of the sentences you need quickly, without having to think about conjugations.

There are many other verbs that can be used with an infinitive to create a two-verb sentence, including the verb "to know something" (explained in the supplemental section) and the verb "should" (explained in Lesson Thirteen). Once you know how the process works, you can easily build fluency, without having to learn lots of rules or exceptions.

Lesson Twelve Expressions

¿Qué va a hacer?	keh BAH-ah-SAI*RR*?	What are You going to do?
Puede hacer eso.	PWAY-theh ah-SAI*RR* EH-soh	You can do that.
Sí, claro.	SEE, CLAH-ddoh	Yes, of course. (clearly)

Speaking Practice

Practice the Lesson Twelve mini-dialogues. Use the lists given. The dialogues will show the "Actions" words as <u>to action</u>, so you remember that these are the infinitive forms. In dialogues B and C you have a choice of responses. Pick a response that makes sense within the conversation.

NOTE: Remember that if the English translation of the infinitive includes a word such as "at," "to," "for," or "how," this means that those words are automatically included in the verb, and you DO NOT need to add them. So, "to listen <u>to</u> music" is simply **escuchar música**. The "to" is already in the verb **escuchar**, which means "to listen <u>to</u>."

In other cases, you will need to add an extra word after the verb (for example, "to go <u>to</u>" is **ir <u>a</u>.**) You will want to pay close attention to the exact meanings of things as you are learning Spanish.

Speaking Activities

1) Pick a dialogue and act it out. Work with a partner, and use props, if possible.
2) Write a dialogue based on the Lesson Twelve mini-dialogues, and use ONLY the vocabulary presented in this lesson and previous lessons.
3) Act out your own dialogue. Work with a partner, and use props, if possible.

More Practice

1) Study the verbs in Lesson Twelve, using the pronunciation guide. Make flashcards or a study list. Work with a partner if you can.
2) Learn the verbs in this lesson by heart.
3) Continue to study your "Actions" words (both basic and specialty).
4) Visit **www.spanishthatworks.org** for additional suggestions, practice materials, and links to other resources.

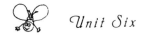

Lesson Twelve Mini-Dialogues:
I want to read!

A) Needing to do something

1) Necesito <u>to action</u>.	1) I need <u>to action</u>.
2) Muy bien.	2) Very well.

ACTIONS: leer un libro, escribir su nombre, usar el teléfono, tomar una clase, regresar mañana, hacer el trabajo, comer, ir a la oficina, OTHER

B) Asking if someone wants or is able to do something

1) Disculpe. ¿(Quiere / Puede) <u>to action</u>?	1) Excuse me. (Do You want/ Can You) <u>to action</u>?
2) (Sí, gracias. / Sí, claro.)	2) (Yes, thanks. / Yes, of course.)
1) (Muy bien. / Gracias. / Vamos.)	1) (Very well. / Thanks. / Let's go.)

ACTIONS: mirar esto, escribir con pluma, usar el teléfono, ir más tarde, ir, comer, tomar la clase, regresar a la oficina, OTHER

C) Asking someone what he or she is going to do

1) ¿Qué va a hacer?	1) What are You going to do?
2) (Voy a hacer esto. / Voy a regresar más tarde.)	2) (I'm going to do this. / I'm going to return later.)

1) Muy bien. Puede hacer eso (en el salón / en la oficina / aquí / allá).	1) Very well. You can do that (in the room / in the office / here / over there).
OR	
1) Muy bien. Puede regresar (al salón / a la oficina / aquí / allá).	1) Very well. You can return (to the room / to the office / here / over there).

EXTRA NOTE:

Some Spanish verbs don't look like English at all in their root form, but add a prefix and they become cognates (related words).

From **tener** / <u>t</u>eh-NAI*RR* (to have), you get **obtener** / ohb-<u>t</u>eh-NAI*RR* (to obtain) and **mantener** / mahn-<u>t</u>eh-NAI*RR* (to maintain).

From **poner** / poh-NAI*RR* (to put), you get **suponer** / soo-poh-NAI*RR* (to suppose) and **componer** / cohm-poh-NAI*RR* (to compose).

Recognizing these related verbs will help you to build your vocabulary.

UNIT SEVEN:

"The meeting is May 20th
at 7:00 p.m."

Lesson 13: How Much?

- ❖ Owe & Should
- ❖ Numbers and Money
- ❖ How to say "Per"
- ❖ Expressions (Minute, hour, let's see...)
- ❖ Mini-Dialogues

Lesson 14: When?

- ❖ Telling the Time
- ❖ The Day
- ❖ The Date
- ❖ How to give a Due Date
- ❖ Expressions (How nice!)
- ❖ Mini-Dialogues

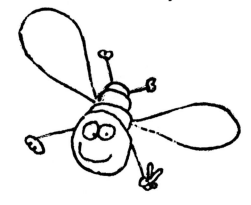

LESSON THIRTEEN: How much?

Basic Structures

A) OWE & SHOULD

The following verb can be very useful.

debo	THEH-boh	I owe, I should
debe	THEH-beh	You, s/he owe, You, s/he should
deben	THEH-behn	You all, they owe, You all, they should

This verb is related to the English word "debt." Its first use is to express money that is owed.

Examples:

¿Cuánto / KWAHN-<u>t</u>oh debo?   How much do I owe?

Ud. debe ocho centavos.   You owe eight cents.

The second use is to express an action that someone should or must do.

Examples:

¿Debo ir ahora?   Should / must I go now?

Usted debe regresar.   You should / must return.

English speakers often use "should" to express a thought that contradicts reality. For example, "I should go" (but I don't). The verb **debo, debe, deben,** however, implies a sense of obligation, similar to "have to" or "must." When used with **de** / theh, it can mean something that <u>must be</u> or <u>probably is</u> true.

Debe de ser / SAIRR Juan.   That must be (probably is) Juan.

Also, in English, we leave out the "to" of the infinitive after verbs like "should." So we say "I should go," not "I should <u>to</u> go." However, in Spanish, you use **debo, debe, deben** with the infinitive verb (-R or –RSE ending), the same as you do with **quiero, necesita,** and the other essential verbs from Lesson Twelve.

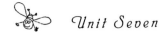

❀❀❀❀❀
Check for Understanding

Owe & Should. Translate to Spanish. Answers are in the supplemental section.

1) You should speak in Spanish.

2) You owe five cents (cinco centavos).

3) I don't owe much (mucho).

4) I must go to the meeting.

B) NUMBERS & MONEY

Now you can apply what you have learned about Spanish pronunciation to the numbers. Be especially careful to say the "th" of "brother" for the "d" in **dos**, **diez**, and **doce** and the flap "r" in **tres** and **cuatro**. Notice that **seis** and **veinte** have an **ei** or "A" sound. **Siete** and **diez** have an **ie** or "yeh" sound. When you count (1,2,3...) you can say **uno** (or **una**), but you must say **un** and **una** if you count items: one pencil (**un lápiz**), twenty-one pens (**veinte y una plumas**), etc.

NUMBERS 1-20

1 uno (un / una)	OO-noh (etc.)	11 once	OHN-seh
2 dos	thohs	12 doce	THOH-seh
3 tres	t'DDEHSS	13 trece	t'DDEH-seh
4 cuatro	KWAH-t'ddoh	14 catorce	kah-TOHRR-seh
5 cinco	SEENG-koh	15 quince	KEEN-seh
6 seis	seyss (sayce)	16 diez y seis	th'YEHSSee SAYCE
7 siete	s'YEH-teh	17 diez y siete	th'YEHSSee s'YEH-teh
8 ocho	OH-choh	18 diez y ocho	th'YEHSSee OH-choh
9 nueve	NWEH-veh	19 diez y nueve	th'YEHSSee NWEH-veh
10 diez	th'YEHSS	20 veinte	BANE-teh, VANE-teh

Spanish uses the word "and" (**y** / **ee**) between the tens and ones in the numbers from 21-99. So, 22 is "twenty and two," (**veinte y dos***), 35 is "thirty and five," (**treinta y cinco**), and 98 is "ninety and eight" (**noventa y ocho**).

*The word for 20 (**veinte**) ends in –E, but 30-90 end in –A (**treinta, cuarenta**, etc.). In speech, the "e" in **veinte** blends with the **y** /**ee**, so 22 is BANE-tee-THOHSS. In some countries, the words for 16-19 and 21-29 are written in a short form (**dieciséis, veintiuno**, etc.).

NUMBERS 21-200

21 veinte y uno (un / una)	BANE-tee OO-noh	70 setenta	seh-TEHN-tah
30 treinta	t'DDANE-tah	80 ochenta	oh-CHEN-tah
33 treinta y tres	t'DDANE-tah-ee t'DDEHS	90 noventa	noh-VEHN-tah
40 cuarenta	kwahddEHN-tah	100 cien	s'YEHN
50 cincuenta	seen-KWEHN-tah	101 ciento uno	s'YEHN-toh OO-noh
60 sesenta	seh-SEHN-tah	200 doscientos	thohs-s'YEHN-tohss

MONEY WORDS

un dólar	oon THOH-lah*rr*	one (a) dollar
dólares	THOH-lahddehs	dollars
centavos	sehn-TAH-vohss	cents

The word **dólar** / THOH-lah*rr* and the plural **dólares** / THOH-lahddehs are both stressed on the FIRST syllable, just like English. The word **dolor** / thoh-LOH*RR*, with the accent on the SECOND syllable, means "pain," so you'll want to practice **dólar** correctly.

Amounts of dollars and cents can be expressed in Spanish as in English:

45¢	cuarenta y cinco centavos	forty-five cents
$1.30	un dólar y treinta centavos	one dollar and thirty cents
$5.00	cinco dólares	five dollars
$10.05	diez dólares y cinco centavos	ten dollars and five cents

❀❀❀❀❀
Check for Understanding

How Much? Practice saying how many dollars and cents something is. Use a study list or the "Numbers, Time, Day, Date" reference sheet to help you.

> Q. ¿Cuánto es?*
>
> A. $2.10, 25¢, $4.45, $1.35, 90¢, $8.05, 15¢

*NOTE: You may also use **¿Cuánto cuesta?** / KWEHS-<u>t</u>ah when you want to ask the price or cost of a specific item that is for sale.

C) HOW TO SAY "PER"

The word **por** can translate as "per" ("per day," "per person," etc.) or as "for" when talking about a POR-tion of time or money, or to express "for receipt of." **Por** is also used in many fixed expressions where the concept of "for" doesn't translate into English at all.

por	POHRR	per, for receipt of, for a POR-tion of time or money, fixed expressions

PER

Es un dólar por cada* minuto.	It's one dollar per (each) minute.
Debe leer quince minutos por día.	You should read 15 min. per day.
Son cinco dólares por todo.*	It's five dollars for everything.

*NOTE: Be sure to pronounce **cada** / CAH-thah and **todo** / <u>T</u>OH-thoh with the "d" as the "th" in "brother."

POR-tion of time or money

diez centavos por la pluma	ten cents for the pen
veinte dólares por el trabajo	twenty dollars for the job
por tres semanas	for three weeks
por ahora	for now

For receipt of

un recibo por la pluma	a receipt for the pen
gracias por las flores	thanks for (receipt of) the flowers

Fixed expressions

por favor	thanks
por ejemplo	for example
por teléfono	on the phone
por aquí	this way

Up to this point in the course, you have mostly been practicing the word **para**, which means "intended for." **Para** can also translate as "to" or "in order to."

The word **por** sounds like the English word "for," but except for a POR-tion of time and money, "for receipt of," and some fixed expressions, <u>most</u> of the time when you want to say "for" someone or something, you will use **para**.

For more explanation of **para** vs. **por**, see the supplemental section.

Lesson Thirteen Expressions

¿Cuánto debo?	KWAHN-<u>t</u>oh THEH-boh?	How much do I owe?
A ver.	ah VAI<i>RR</i>	Let's see.
Aquí lo tiene.	ah-KEE loh <u>T</u>YEH-neh	Here you are (have it).
quisiera	kee-s'YEHddah	I'd like
pagar	pah-GAH<i>RR</i>	to pay
por todo	poh<i>rr</i> <u>T</u>OH-thoh	for everything, all
minuto	mee-NOO-<u>t</u>oh	minute
hora	OH-ddah	hour
día (m.)	THEE-ah	day
semana	seh-MAH-nah	week

 ### Speaking Practice

Practice the Lesson Thirteen mini-dialogues. Work with a partner, if possible.
1) For all the dialogues, the places to insert numbers and dollar amounts are indicated by an "X." Use the money amounts listed, and then make up your own. Use the "Numbers, Time, Day, Date" reference sheet or a study list to help you.
2) For the "should" dialogues, choose an action word that fits the context. For example, you might say **Debe** <u>usar</u> **el teléfono**, **Debe** <u>regresar</u> **a su casa**, **Debe** <u>ir</u> **a la junta**, etc. Use your "Actions" words from Lesson Eleven to come up with other possibilities.

Speaking Activities

1) Pick a dialogue and act it out. Work with a partner, and use props, if possible.
2) Write a dialogue based on the Lesson Thirteen mini-dialogues, and use ONLY the vocabulary presented in this lesson and previous lessons.
3) Act out your own dialogue. Work with a partner, and use props, if possible.

More Practice

1) Practice saying the numbers 1-101, (plus 200), and the Lesson Thirteen structures and expressions aloud, using the pronunciation guide. Work with a partner.
2) Learn the Lesson Thirteen structures and expressions by heart.
3) Start learning the numbers 1-100. It will take time before you can be really fluent in numbers, so keep your study list or "Numbers, Time, Day, Date" reference sheet handy. In real-life conversation, remember that you can always write the numbers down for people until you're confident.
4) Visit **www.spanishthatworks.org** for additional suggestions, practice materials, and links to other resources.

Lesson Thirteen Mini-Dialogues:
How much?

A) Asking how much one owes

1) Perdón, ¿cuánto debo?	1) Excuse me. How much do I owe?
2) A ver. *(Looks it up.)* X (dólar / dólares / centavos) por todo.	2) Let's see. *(Looks it up.)* X (dollar / dollars / cents) for everything.
1) Aquí lo tiene.	1) Here you are (Here you have it).
2) Gracias.	2) Thanks

AMOUNTS: $3.10, 45¢, $4.25, $70, 78¢, $6.05, 20¢, $10.00, 85¢

B) Paying something

1) Quisiera pagar.	1) I'd like to pay.
2) Muy bien. (X) dólares, por favor.	2) Very well. (X) dollars, please.
1) Aquí lo tiene.	1) Here you are (Here you have it).
2) Gracias. ¿Hay algo más?	2) Thanks. Is there anything else?
1) No, nada más, gracias.	1) No, nothing more, thanks.

AMOUNTS: cinco, diez, veinte, treinta, cuarenta, cincuenta, sesenta, setenta, ochenta, noventa, cien

C) Saying what someone should do & when

1) Debe (ir / regresar) (a su casa / a la junta / al trabajo / a la oficina).	1) You should (go / return) (to your house / to the meeting / to work / to the office).
2) ¿Cuándo?	2) When?
1) En X (minutos / horas / días / semanas).	1) In X (minutes / hours / days / weeks).

TIME AMOUNTS: cinco minutos, quince minutos, una hora, dos horas, dos días, cinco días, una semana, dos semanas

EXTRA NOTE:

Bargaining the price is common practice in
Latino markets and outdoor fairs.

Just repeat back the original price with surprise
and then offer a smaller amount:

¿Diez? / th'yehss? **Es mucho.** / MOO-choh
Le doy cinco. / lay thoy SEENG-koh
(Ten??? It's too much. I give you five.)

In regular stores, you usually pay the price
marked on the item, but there may be room to
negotiate under special circumstances.

LESSON FOURTEEN: When?

Basic Structures

A) TELLING THE TIME

In English, we express time as the numbers "of the clock" (o'clock). In Spanish, time is expressed as hours. You use **la** and **las** with a number to show that you are talking about time because the word for "hour" (**hora**) is feminine.

1:00	la una		7:00	las siete
2:00	las dos		8:00	las ocho
3:00	las tres		9:00	las nueve
4:00	las cuatro		10:00	las diez
5:00	las cinco		11:00	las once
6:00	las seis		12:00	las doce

With all the plural numbers (2-12) you say **las** before the number. The number is the same as when you count. You do NOT add –S to the number.

"One o'clock" is special. Because it is singular, you say **la**. And since "hour" (**hora**) is feminine, you use the feminine form for "one" (**una**).

There are several ways to express minutes past the hour in Spanish. The <u>easiest</u> way is to say the hour (**la una, las dos, tres, cuatro,** etc.), the word "and" (**y** / ee), and then the minutes (**quince, veinte y cinco, treinta y cinco, cincuenta**).

(la / las) (<u>hour</u>) y /ee (<u>minutes</u>)

The "and" (**y**/ ee) is usually left out after the hour in the minutes from 31-59.

(la / las) (<u>hour</u>) (<u>minutes</u>)

Examples:

1:15	la una y quince		4:35	las cuatro treinta y cinco
2:25	las dos y veinte y cinco		8:50	las ocho cincuenta

Speakers sometimes say **cuarto** / KWAHRR-toh, (¼) instead of 15, and <u>usually</u> say **media** / MEH-th'yah, (½) instead of 30, when talking about time.

cuarto	KWAHRR-toh	15 min. before / after
media	MEH-th'yah	30 min. after the hour

Examples:

1:15	la una y cuarto	2:30	las dos y media
3:15	las tres y cuarto	1:30	la una y media

In order to talk about a specific hour in the a.m. or p.m., Spanish speakers talk about time "in the morning" and time "in the afternoon." After dark, (or about 9:00 p.m. or so), you can talk about time "at night."

de la mañana	theh lah mahn-YAH-nah	a.m., specific hour in the morning
de la tarde	theh lah TAHRR-theh	p.m., specific hour in afternoon or evening
de la noche	theh lah NOH-cheh	p.m., specific hour at night, bedtime

Examples

7:15 a.m.	las siete y cuarto de la mañana	7:30 p.m.	las siete y media de la tarde
1:00 p.m.	la una de la tarde	10:00 p.m.	las diez de la noche

Extra Expressions

Native speakers from other areas may express time in different ways, but they will understand you if you use this method. Some other words you may hear are **menos** / MEH-nohss (for "minus" minutes before the hour), **para** / PAHddah (for minutes "to" the hour), and **en punto** / ehn POON-toh (for the hour "sharp"). The 24 hour (military style) clock is sometimes used for public events such as train schedules, TV programs, and concerts.

1:45	quince para las dos	2:40	las tres menos veinte
9:00 sharp	las nueve en punto	7:00 p.m.	las diecinueve horas

The time now vs. the time of an event

To ask what time it is <u>now</u>, you say **¿Qué hora es?** / kay-OHddah ehss (What hour is it?)

To answer what the time is <u>now</u>, the easiest way is to just say **la** or **las** and then the numbers: **la una y quince, las cuatro y veinte, las ocho,** etc.

Grammar texts usually make you say the verb when you give the time now. For example, they make you say "It is four twenty" (**Son las cuatro y veinte**), or "It is one thirty" (**Es la una y media**), when you say the time.

However, making the complete sentence is NOT necessary in conversation, and can cause confusion later on, when you want to say <u>at</u> what time something is happening. When someone asks you the time <u>now</u>, the easiest way to answer is to just say the hour (and minutes, if there are any), without any extras.

¿Qué hora es?	kay OHddah EHSS?	What time (hour) is it? (now)
Las tres.	lahss t'ddehss	Three o'clock.

Giving the time is slightly different if you want to ask the time of an event, and <u>not</u> just the time right now. To ask <u>at</u> what time an event is happening, you say **¿A qué hora es?** / ah keh OHddah ehss? ("At" what time is it?)

Similarly, to say what time something is happening, you say **a** / ah and then the hour (a /ah **la una y quince,** a /ah **las cuatro y veinte,** a /ah **las ocho** etc.)

¿A qué hora es?	AH keh Ohddah EHSS?	"At" what time is (the event) going to be?
A las tres.	ah lahss-t'DDEHSS	"At" three o'clock.

NOTE: the word **a** / ah in Spanish means "to," as in "I am going <u>to</u> the house" (**Voy <u>a</u> la casa**). We don't talk about things being "to" a certain time in English, so the closest translation for **a** / ah when you talk about the hour is "at."

Remember that to say where something is physically "at," you use the word **en** (in, on, at): **Estoy en la casa** (I'm at the house).

🌸🌸🌸🌸🌸
Check for Understanding

Time. Practice giving the time "now," vs. saying "at" what time the meeting is.

Example: 11:00

<u>What time is it (**now**)?</u>	<u>What time is the meeting (**at**)?</u>
Q1. ¿Qué hora es?	Q2. ¿A qué hora es la junta?
A1. Las once.	A2. **A** las once.

PRACTICE: 1:15, 9:15, 4:10, 3:30, 7:50, 8:20, 12:05, 11:10

B) THE DAY

To ask about the day of the week, you say **¿Qué día es?** / kay THEE-ah ehss? (What day is it?)

The Days of the Week

¿Qué día es?	kay THEE-ah ehss?	What day is it?
lunes	LOO-nehss	Monday
martes	MAHRR-tehss	Tuesday
miércoles	M'YEHRR-coh-lehss	Wednesday
jueves	HWEH-vehss	Thursday
viernes	V'YEHRR-nehss	Friday
sábado	SAH-bah-thoh	Saturday
domingo	thoh-MEENG-goh	Sunday

NOTE: The Spanish calendar week begins with Monday.

As in English, Monday is named after the Moon (Luna). Tuesday through Friday derive from the Latin words for Mars, Mercury, Jupiter (Jove), and Venus. The words for Saturday and Sunday are related to the English words Sabbath, and Dominican.

Please note that the days of the week are NOT capitalized in Spanish and that all of the days of the week except **domingo** are stressed on the FIRST syllable.

Asking what day it is, or what day something is on

To ask what day something is on, you can just ask **¿Qué día es?**

To answer what day something is "on," you don't use the word for physically being "on" or "in" something (en). If you say you arrived **en lunes**, a Spanish speaker might ask you, "Who's Lunes, your donkey?"

In Spanish, to talk about what day something is "on," you say **el** and then the day. You use the masculine form **el** because the word for "day" is masculine: <u>**el día**</u>. (There are quite a few common words ending in –A which are masculine, including "the day" /**el día** and "the problem" / **el problema**).

To talk about what days something is "on" (for an ongoing event, such as a class) you say **los** (the) and the plural form of the day. You add an –S to **sábado** and **domingo** for the plural. The other days of the week have the same form for both singular and plural.

Examples:

el lunes	ehl LOO-nehss	"on" Monday
el sábado	ehl SAH-bah-thoh	"on" Saturday
los lunes	lohs LOO-nehss	"on" Mondays
los sábados	lohs SAH-bah-thohs	"on" Saturdays

As you can see, words such as "on," "at," and "to" may not translate word for word from English. You use the word "to" (**a** / ah) to say what time something is <u>at</u>, and you use the word "the" (**el, los**) to express what day something is <u>on</u>. Because they often don't translate directly, words such as "on," "at," and "to" are best learned in context.

Check for Understanding

"On" Sunday. Translate to Spanish. Answers are in the supplemental section.

on Sunday, on Tuesdays, on Friday, on Mondays and Wednesdays, on Thursday, on Saturdays and Sundays

Check for Understanding

When? Practice saying <u>when</u> a class is: what day or days, and at what time. Use **el** for a one-time event, and **los** for an ongoing event. Look at the schedule and follow the dialogue. Remember: when you talk about **la hora** (the hour), you use **la** or **las**. When you talk about **el día** (the day), you use **el** or **los**. Answers are in the supplemental section.

Children's class: Thursdays, 8:00 a.m.	Music class: Saturday, 2:00 p.m.
Internet: Wednesday, 9:30 a.m.	English: Fridays, 6:30 p.m.
Computers: Mondays, 10:00 a.m.	Spanish: Tues. & Thurs., 3:00 p.m.

Q. ¿Cuándo es la clase de (niños / Internet-een-*tai rr*-NEH<u>T</u> / computadoras / música / inglés / español)?

A1. El <u>day of week</u> a /ah (la /las) <u>X</u> de / theh la (mañana / tarde).

OR

A2. **Los** <u>days of week</u> a /ah (la /las) <u>X</u> de /theh la (mañana / tarde).

C) THE DATE

To ask what the date is, you say **¿Cuál es la fecha?** / kwahl-ehss lah FEH-chah? (What / Which is the date?) NOTE: **Fecha** is only used for a calendar date. For a date to meet with another person, use the word **cita** / SEE-<u>t</u>ah (appointment).

The names of the months are easy to recognize and understand in Spanish, because they are cognates (related words).

However, it can be challenging to pronounce the names of the months correctly because they look so much like English. Remember that the "dd" in the pronunciation guide is to be said QUICKLY, to mimic the flap "r." So, the sound **-bre** / b'ddeh is like the French word "bidet," said very fast. Also, be sure to say an "s" sound for the "z" in **marzo**.

The Months of the Year

enero	eh-NEHddoh	January
febrero	feh-b'DDEHddoh	February
marzo	MAH*RR*-soh	March
abril	ah-b'ddEEL	April
mayo	MAH-yoh	May
junio	HOON-yoh	June
julio	HOOL-yoh	July
agosto	ah-GOHS-<u>t</u>oh	August
septiembre	sehp-<u>t</u>'YEHM-b'ddeh	September
octubre	ohk-<u>T</u>OO-b'ddeh	October
noviembre	noh-v'YEHM-b'ddeh	November
diciembre	thee-s'YEHM-b'ddeh	December

Like the days of the week, the months are NOT capitalized in Spanish. The Spanish word for "month" is **mes** (m.) / mehss.

Giving the date

The date is given in Spanish using the form "the <u>day</u> of <u>month</u>." For the day, you usually just use the regular cardinal numbers 2, 3, 4, and not the ordinal numbers 2nd, 3rd, 4th, etc.

The exception is the first day of the month, for which you can use the word **primero** / p'ddee-MEHddoh (first).

el / ehl (<u>number of day</u>) de / theh (<u>month</u>)

Examples:

July 4th	el cuatro de julio
November 20th	el veinte de noviembre
May 5th	el cinco de mayo
Jan. 1st	el primero de enero

Asking what date something is on

To ask what date something is on, you can say **¿En qué fecha?** / ehn keh FEH-chah? (On what date?). You can also ask **¿Cuándo?** / KWAHN-thoh (When?)

¿Cuál es la fecha?	KWAHL-ehss-lah FEH-chah?	What's the date?
¿En qué fecha es…?	ehn keh FEH-chah ehss…?	On what date is….?
¿Cuándo es…?	KWAHN-thoh ehss…?	When is…?

To say what date, both the date "today" and the date something is "on," use **el** / ehl (the).

Examples:

¿Cuál es la fecha?   What is the date (today)?
El treinta de enero.   January 30th.
¿En qué fecha es la junta?   On what date is the meeting?
El tres de agosto.   "On" August 3rd.
¿Cuándo es la junta?   When is the meeting?
El veinte de abril.   "On" April 20th.

NOTE: in Spanish the date is written numerically the same way it is spoken, so 5-3 is March 5th. If you are writing out dates in English for Spanish speakers, it is best to write out the month (Feb. 8, Jan. 2, Mar. 5) in order to avoid confusion.

Check for Understanding

Date. Practice saying the following dates. Use the formula **el _____ de _____**.

Answers are in the supplemental section.

February 17, August 3, October 22, January 8, March 2, July 19, June 8

D) HOW TO GIVE A DUE DATE

Spanish doesn't have an easy translation for "due by," but the following expressions will convey the same meaning.

antes de	AHN-tehss theh	before
antes del	AHN-tehss thehl	before the (day, date)
antes de (la / las)	AHN-tehss theh (lah / lass)	before the (time)
para	PAH-ddah	intended for (due by)*
fecha de vencimiento	FEH-chah theh vehn-see-m'YEHN-toh	expiration date, due date

*NOTE: **Para** is used to talk about a specific <u>intended</u> date, not a POR-tion of time. For more explanation, please see the supplemental section.

Examples:

Necesita ir antes del diez de marzo.	You need to go before March 10th.
Favor de regresar esto antes del martes.	Please return this before Tuesday.
Tiene que regresar antes de las cinco.	You have to return before five o'clock.
Es para el jueves.	It's for (due by) Thursday.
La fecha de vencimiento es el doce de junio.	The due date is June 12th.

Lesson Fourteen Expressions

¿Cuándo?	KWAHN-thoh?	When?
Ya me voy	yah meh VOY	I'm leaving now
cumpleaños (m.)	coom-play-AHN-yohss	birthday
¡Qué bueno!	keh-BWEH-noh!	How nice!

NOTE: Be sure to pronounce the ñ in **cumpleaños** with the "ny" of "canyon."

Speaking Practice

Practice the Lesson Fourteen mini-dialogues. Work with a partner, if possible.
1) For all the dialogues, the places to insert numbers are indicated by an "<u>X</u>."
Use the list below each dialogue for times and dates.
2) In dialogue B, you can mix and match. Remember: hours are feminine (**la / las**) and days are masculine (**el / los**).
3) For dialogue C, use the list of dates given, and then improvise with the birthdays of people you know.
4) You can continue the conversation in dialogue C by talking about friends or family members who have similar birthdays. Use this phrase:

El cumpleaños de mi (<u>hermano, amigo, mamá</u>, etc.) **es el ___ de ____.**

Speaking Activities

1) Pick a dialogue and act it out with a partner in front of the class.
2) Write a dialogue based on the Lesson Fourteen mini-dialogues, and use ONLY the vocabulary presented in this lesson and previous lessons.
3) Act out your own dialogue. Work with a partner, and use props, if possible.

More Practice

1) Practice saying the hours, days, and months aloud, using the pronunciation guide. Make a study list or use the "Numbers, Time, Day, Date" reference sheet. Work with a partner, if possible.
2) Begin learning the hours, days, and months by heart. Keep your study list or reference sheet handy until you know the time words well.
3) Visit **www.spanishthatworks.org** for additional suggestions, practice materials, and links to other resources.

©2009 Almann ~ Spanish that Works™ ~ www.spanishthatworks.org

Lesson Fourteen Mini-Dialogues:
When?

A) Asking the time

1) Disculpe. ¿Qué hora es?	1) Excuse me. What time is it?
2) (La / Las) <u>X</u>.	2) <u>X</u> (o'clock).
1) Ah, (muchas gracias. / ya me voy).	1) Oh, (thanks a lot / I'm leaving now).

HOURS: 8:20, 1:15, 2:30, 11:50, 5:45,
9:05, 12:10, 10:40, 3:30, 6:55, 1:20, 7:50

B) Asking when classes are

1) Perdón. ¿Cuándo es la clase de (inglés / español / computadoras)?	1) Excuse me. When is the (English / Spanish / computer) class?
2) (El / los) <u>day(s)</u> a (la/las) <u>X</u>.	2) On <u>day(s)</u> at <u>X</u> (o'clock).
1) Muchas gracias.	1) Thanks a lot.

DAY & TIMES: Monday 8:00 p.m., Saturdays 1:00, Friday 11:15,
Tues. / Thursdays 2:30, Wednesdays 5:45, Sunday 9:00 a.m.

C) Talking about birthdays

1) ¿Cuándo es su cumpleaños?	1) When is Your birthday?
2) El <u>day</u> de <u>month</u>. ¿Y su cumpleaños?	2) The <u>day</u> of <u>month</u>. And Your birthday?
1) El <u>day</u> de <u>month</u>.	1) The <u>day</u> of <u>month</u>.
2) ¡Qué bueno!	2) How nice!

DATES: Sept. 13, Feb. 5, Oct. 20, Nov. 18, Mar. 8, May 1,
Jan. 2, Apr. 17, June 26, July 12, Aug. 16, Dec. 31

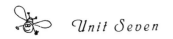

EXTRA NOTE:

Latino culture has its own way of judging
what it means to be "on time."

For social engagements, people often have a
more relaxed attitude about time, and tardiness
is tolerated. In some cases, it may be expected
that people will arrive a little bit late, and arriving
early might be seen as an imposition.

However, people generally arrive on time for
business appointments, performances, etc.

To clarify that punctuality will be a priority,
use this expression after the hour:

En punto / ehn POON-<u>t</u>oh (Sharp)

UNIT EIGHT:

"How may I help you?"

Lesson 15: Getting Information

- ❖ Names
- ❖ Numbers (Phone, ID...)
- ❖ Addresses
- ❖ Expressions (What is Your...?)
- ❖ Mini-Dialogues

Lesson 16: Building Vocabulary

- ❖ Endings & the Parts of Speech
- ❖ Past Participle: -ADO / -IDO (-ADA / -IDA)
- ❖ Been There, Done That: Verbs
- ❖ Describing Things: Adjectives
- ❖ Naming Things: Nouns
- ❖ Expressions (So long, good luck...)
- ❖ Mini-Dialogues

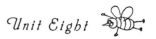

LESSON FIFTEEN: Getting Information

Basic Structures

A) NAMES

Look at these two questions.

¿Qué es esto?	KAY-ehss EH-s<u>t</u>oh?	What is this?
Es un libro.	EHssoon LEE-b'ddoh	It's a book.
¿Cuál es su nombre?	KWAHL-ehs-soo-NOHM-b'ddeh?	What is Your name?
Mi nombre es Ana.	mee NOHM-b'ddeh ehss AH-nah	My name is Ana.

¿Qué es? asks for a <u>name</u> of something, or for a <u>definition</u>.

¿Cuál es? is used to ask for all kinds of personal <u>information</u>, such as name, telephone number, and address. **¿Cuál?** means "Which?" so in a way, you are saying, "Which is your name (phone number, address, etc.)?"

NOTE: You may also be familiar with **¿Cómo se llama?** / KOH-moh seh YAH-mah?, which literally translates as "How do You call yourself?" The answer, **Me llamo Ana** /may YAH-moh AH-nah, means "I call myself Ana."

¿Cómo se llama? can also mean "How is it called?" as if an inanimate object could call itself something. The grammar is based on the verb **llamarse** (to call oneself), and is often misunderstood by English speakers. In this lesson, you will be practicing the direct translation of "name," which is **nombre**.

Given names and family names in Spanish

Spanish speakers use more given names and family names than English speakers, and it can be a challenge to get a Spanish speaker's name to fit into the "first name—middle initial—last name" system that is used for filing purposes in the United States. In fact, the entire concept of "first" and "last" names loses all meaning in Spanish. It's better to think of <u>main</u> names.

For example, Mexican painter Diego Rivera's complete name was **José Diego Rivera Barrientos**, but he would never have called himself **José Barrientos**. His <u>main</u> names were "Diego" and "Rivera."

Spanish speakers outside the United States usually use two family names for formal purposes: the father's surname, and the mother's maiden surname. The father's surname is considered to be the <u>main</u> surname, or what an English speaker would call a "last name." However, the mother's maiden name is written last. This leads to a lot of confusion with English speakers, because a person might <u>write</u> the complete name, but <u>tell</u> you only the father's surname.

In many Latino countries, a married woman may keep her father's surname for legal purposes, but use her husband's name in social situations by adding the word **de** / theh (of, from) and the husband's main surname. For example, Mexican painter Frida Kahlo's complete name was **Magdalena Carmen Frida Kahlo Calderón**. Because she was married to Diego Rivera, she might have called herself **Magdalena Carmen Frida Kahlo Calderón de Rivera**. The "de" may be omitted with a title ("señora Rivera"), and is usually dropped if the woman takes the husband's name for legal purposes.

As with **José Diego** and **Magdalena Carmen Frida**, it is common for people to use their second (or third!) given name as their "first" (main) name, especially among those whose name starts with María or José. It is also common to use two given names as the main name, so a woman named **María Elena Padilla** might consider her "first" (main) name to be "María Elena."

In order to alphabetize a Spanish name, you must determine the main surname, which is usually the surname of the father. One way to be sure of the name is to ask for the **apellido paterno** / ah-peh-YEE-thoh pah-<u>T</u>AI<i>RR</i>-noh (paternal surname). Another is to say the first and last name back to the person. For example, if a man writes **Roberto Gómez Torres**, and you're not sure what the main surname is, ask ¿**Es usted Roberto Gómez o Roberto Torres?**

In Latin America, the answer would be "Roberto Gómez," but Spanish speakers in the U.S. sometimes choose to use the mother's maiden name as the middle name, hyphenate the father and mother's surnames, or drop the mother's name entirely, so it can be a good idea to check.

Check for Understanding

Names. Write out your own name as it would be in a Spanish-speaking country. Fill in the blanks. Married women may fill in the 5th blank.

Q. ¿Cuál es su nombre?
A. _____

_____	_____	_____	_____
First name	Middle name	Father's surname	Mother's maiden

de _____
Husband's main surname

B) TELEPHONE NUMBERS

¿Cuál es su número de teléfono?	KWAHL-ehss soo NOO-mehddoh theh <u>t</u>eh-LEH-foh-noh?	What is Your telephone number?
¿Cuál es el número de teléfono de... ?	KWAHL-ehss ehl NOO-mehddoh theh...?	What is the number of (for) the...?
Es el...	ehs EHL	It's...

In Spanish, telephone numbers are read in pairs. When there are 3 digits in a grouping, the first number is read as a single digit, and then the remaining two numbers are read as a double digit number. (The exception is with zeroes, which are usually read as single digits to avoid confusion.)

So, (480) 377-5164 would be read as:

(4—80)	3—77	51	64
cuatro—ochenta	tres—setenta y siete	cincuenta y uno	sesenta y cuatro

If you read all the numbers as single digits (as in English), you will be understood, but it's a good idea to learn to say important numbers the correct way.

When a zero begins a pair, you always read the zero as a single digit. To be extra clear, you may also read the zero as a single digit at the end of a pair. "Zero" in Spanish is **cero** / SEH-ddoh. The letter "O" is <u>never</u> used for a zero.

So, (602) 982-7042 would be read as:

(6—0—2)	9—82	7—0	42
seis—cero—dos	nueve—ochenta y dos	setenta OR siete—cero	cuarenta y dos

Check for Understanding

Numbers. Write out two phone numbers as you would read them in Spanish. Please note that the word "the" is often used with a telephone number ("el," because **número** is masculine). Also, you do not <u>have</u> to say "It is…" to give your phone number, but speakers often do, so it is included here for practice.

> Q. ¿Cuál es su número de teléfono? (What's your phone number?)
> A. Es el… (It's…)

(_____) _____ _____

(_____) _____ _____

C) OTHER NUMBERS

número de identificación	NOO-mehddoh. theh ee-then-<u>t</u>ee-fee-cah-s'YOHN	ID number (can be used for PIN)
número de seguro social	NOO-mehddoh theh seh-GOO-ddoh soh-s'YAHL	Social security number

ID numbers are read in pairs, like telephone numbers. So, 518-62-3375 would be read **cinco, diez y ocho, sesenta y dos, treinta y tres, setenta y cinco.** Of course, you would also be understood if you read the numbers as single digits.

Numbers with decimals are given using the word **punto** / POON-toh (point). So, "58.1" is **cincuenta y ocho punto uno**. (NOTE: In some countries, a comma is used for the decimal point, and a point is used for the comma.)

When you are first learning a language, and especially if it is important for you to be accurate, the best way to express large numbers is to write them down. The numerals are the same in both languages!

D) ADDRESSES

¿Cuál es su dirección?	KWAHL-ehss soo thee-ddek-s'YOHN?	What is Your address?
Calle _____, número (X).	KAH-yeh _____, NOO-mehhdoh (X).	Street _____, number (X).
Avenida _____, número (X).	ah-veh-NEE-thah _____, NOO-mehhdoh (X).	Avenue _____, number (X).

As you can see, in Spanish you say **calle** (Street) or **avenida** (Avenue) first, and then the street name. Then you say **número** (number) and the street number.

Street numbers above one hundred may be read as one large number. For example:

Calle Clark, número ciento veinte y tres   123 Clark Street

In Latin America, large street numbers are often given paired, as with telephone numbers. You could also read a street number as single digits if necessary, and you would still be understood.

Avenida Oak, número sesenta y dos, treinta y ocho   6238 Oak Avenue

Check for Understanding

Address. Write out your address as you would read it in Spanish.

Q. ¿Cuál es su dirección?

A. (Calle/ Avenida)_____ , número _____.

More Address Words

norte	NOH*RR*-teh	North
sur	SOO*RR*	South
este	EH-s<u>t</u>eh	East
oeste	oh-EH-s<u>t</u>eh	West

Lesson Fifteen Expressions

¿Cuál es (su / el / la)...?	KWAHL-ehss (soo / ehl / lah)...?	What is (Your, his, her. their / the)...?

nombre (m.)	NOHM-b'ddeh	(given) name
...y apellido	ee ah-peh-YEE-thoh	...and surname
...del* padre	thehl PAH-th'ddeh	...of the father
...de la madre	theh lah MAH-th'ddeh	...of the mother
apellido paterno	ah-peh-YEE-thoh pah-<u>T</u>AI*RR*-noh	father's surname

número	NOO-mehddoh	number
...de teléfono	theh <u>t</u>eh-LEH-foh-noh	...of telephone
...de identificación	theh ee-then-<u>t</u>ee-fee-cah s'YOHN	...of identification
...de trabajo	theh <u>t</u>'ddah-BAH-hoh	...at your job (work #)

dirección (f.)	thee-ddek-s'YOHN	address
edad (f.)	eh-THATH	age
fecha de nacimiento**	FEH-chah theh nah-see-m'YEHN-<u>t</u>oh	date of birth

¿En qué puedo servirle?	ehn keh PWEH-thoh sai*rr*-VEE*RR*-leh?	How may I help You?
Eso es.	EH-soh ehss	That's it.
o sea	oh-SAY-ah	or rather, I mean
Muchas gracias.	MOO-chass g'DDAH-s'yahss	Thank you very much.

*The word **del** is a contraction without apostrophe of **de** + **el** and means "of the." The other contraction in Spanish is **a** + **el** (**al**) which means "to the."

**In Spanish the year is always given as a complete number (1999 is read as "one thousand nine hundred and ninety-nine"), so you will not practice date of birth in the dialogues.

Speaking Practice

Practice the Lesson Fifteen mini-dialogues. Work with a partner, if possible.
1) For dialogue A, first give your own information that you wrote in the "Check for Understanding" sections and then fill in the blanks with other names and numbers. Practice this dialogue several times. NOTE: Spanish speakers often use the expression **o sea** / oh-SAY-ah (or rather, I mean, "like," "um," etc.) as a filler word. For other filler expressions, see Lesson Ten.
2) For dialogue B, use your "Things" words to fill in the first "item" blank, and the names on the list or the names of people you know for the second blank.

Speaking Activities

1) Pick a dialogue and act it out. Work with a partner, and use props, if possible.
2) If you are in a class, go around the room interviewing your classmates (dialogue A) or requesting something (dialogue B).
3) Write your own dialogue based on the Lesson Fifteen mini-dialogues.
4) Act out your own dialogue. Work with a partner, and use props, if possible.

More Practice

1) Practice saying the Lesson Fifteen expressions, using the pronunciation guide. Work with a partner. Begin learning the Lesson Fifteen expressions by heart.
2) Visit **www.spanishthatworks.org** for additional practice materials.
3) Review the question words **who, what, which, when, where,** and **how.** Know that sometimes the question word won't translate exactly into English. Also, note that Spanish question words are written with accent marks. You may wish to make a study list or flashcards for the question words.

Question Words

¿Quién?	k'YEHN?	Who?
¿Qué?	KEH?	What? (definition)
¿Cuál?	k'WAHL?	What? (personal info), Which? (choice)
¿Cuándo?	k'WHAN-thoh?	When?
¿Dónde?	THOHN-theh?	Where?
¿Cómo?	COH-moh?	How? What? (you didn't hear)

Lesson Fifteen Mini-Dialogues: Getting Information

A) Getting & giving information

1) ¿Cuál es su nombre y apellido, por favor?	1) What is Your given name and surname, please?
2) <u>Name surname 1 surname 2</u>.	2) *Fill in* <u>name surname 1 surname 2</u>.
1) O sea, ¿<u>name surname 1</u>?	1) Or rather, <u>name surname 1</u>?
2) Sí. Eso es.	2) Yes, that's it.
1) Muy bien. ¿Cuál es su número de teléfono?	1) Very well. What is Your phone number?
2) Es el <u>phone #</u>.	2) It's <u>phone #</u>.
1) Y ¿cuál es su dirección?	1) And, what is Your address?
2) (Calle / Avenida) <u>street name</u>, número (<u>X</u>).	2) (<u>X</u>) <u>street name</u> (Street / Avenue).
1) Muchas gracias.	1) Thank you very much.

Name - surname 1 - surname 2 _____

Phone # (write out numbers) _____

Address (names & numbers) _____

B) Asking for something for someone else

1) ¿En qué puedo servirle?	1) How may I help You?
2) Necesito (el / la / un / una) <u>item</u> para mi (hijo / hija / amigo).	2) I need (the / an) <u>item</u> for my (son /daughter / friend).
1) Muy bien. ¿Cuál es el nombre de su (hijo / hija / amigo)?	1) Very well. What is the name of Your (son / daughter / friend)?
2) _____.	2) _____.
1) Un momento, por favor.	1) One moment, please.

NAMES: Miguel Villa, Leticia Rodríguez, Alejandro Guzmán, Guadalupe García, Roberto Torres, Lucía Gracia, Manuel Castillo, Carmen López, Jorge Flores

EXTRA NOTE:

Remember that you do not always
have to speak in a complete sentence
in order to communicate with someone.

For example, instead of saying
¿Cuál es su nombre? (What is your name?),
you can just look at someone and say
¿Nombre, por favor? (Name, please?).

The more you learn to express yourself with
simple words and structures, the easier it will be
for you to build fluency in the language.

LESSON SIXTEEN: Building Vocabulary

Basic Structures

A) ENDINGS AND THE PARTS OF SPEECH

As you learn more Spanish, you will notice that some new words may look familiar to you, but have slightly different endings from what you have learned.

For example, let's say you hear someone talking about the telephone, and wanting to **hacer una llamada** / yah-MAH-thah. The word **llamada** is unfamiliar to you, but it looks a little like the verb **llamar** / yah-MAHRR (to call).

When confronted with a new word, it's helpful to know the part of speech, or how the word is used in a sentence. You would need to ask yourself: Is the person is expressing an <u>action</u> (verb), <u>describing</u> something (adjective), or <u>naming</u> something (noun)?

In this case, the person is <u>naming something</u> that he or she wants to make, so you know that **llamada** is a noun. You might then be able to deduce from the context that **hacer una llamada** means "to make a telephone call."

You often use related forms of words in English. For example, look at these sentences based on the verbs **use, write,** and **speak:**

I have... **used, written, spoken.** (VERBS)

It is... **used, written, spoken.** (ADJECTIVES)

There is... **use, writing, speech.** (NOUNS)

Check for Understanding

Part of Speech. Say whether the underlined word is expressing <u>action</u> (verb), <u>describing</u> a thing (adjective), or <u>naming</u> a thing that you have (noun).

1) I want <u>to use</u> the phone.   3) The book is <u>used</u>.

2) I have (the) <u>use</u> of the office.   4) I <u>have used</u> the paper.

B) PAST PARTICIPLE ENDINGS: –ADO /–IDO (–ADA /–IDA)

It is common to see Spanish words ending in –**ADO** /AH-thoh, –**IDO** / EE-thoh, –**ADA** /AH-thah, and –**IDA** / EE-thah.

Most of the words with these endings derive from the **past participle**, which is a word based on a verb that can be used either with "have" (to talk about things you have done), or with "is" (to describe things). Spanish also has many noun forms related to the past participle. In English, the regular past participle ending is –**ED** or –**EN** (**used, written, spoken**, etc.).

Your first task is to learn how to pronounce the Spanish past participle endings correctly. Remember, the Spanish "d" is pronounced like the soft "th" sound in "brother": –**ADO** /AH-thoh, –**IDO** / EE-thoh, –**ADA** /AH-thah, –**IDA** / EE-thah.

If you pronounce the "d" as in the English word "soda," a Spanish-speaker will hear an "r" sound (-ARO, -IRO, -ARA, -IRA), and will have to work harder to figure out what you are trying to say. If you say the "d" correctly, you will not only be more easily understood, but you will also understand others better.

Check for Understanding

Sound check. Write out the pronunciation guide for these words. Start each syllable with a <u>consonant</u>, and refer to Lesson One "Saying & Understanding" as needed. Say the words aloud. If possible, ask a Spanish speaker to listen to you and correct your pronunciation. Answers are in the supplemental section.

1) **salida** (exit)

2) **ocupado, ocupada** (busy, occupied)

3) **bebida** (beverage)

4) **han hablado** (they have spoken)

5) **comida** (food)

6) **he comido** (I have eaten)

NOTE: As you may have noticed, a change in ending can change the translated meaning of a word. **Comida** is "food," while **comido** is "eaten." They are related concepts, but used differently in speech. As you build your vocabulary, you will want to pay special attention to word endings. See the supplemental section for more information about learning new vocabulary and recognizing verbs in other tenses.

Forming the past participle

Past participles are made from infinitive verbs, such as the ones you studied in Lesson Eleven. In Spanish, the past participle is easy to make. You just take off the infinitive endings (-AR, -ER, -IR) and make the following substitutions:

–ADO / AH-thoh for an **–AR** ending

mirar--> mir**ado** / meeDDAH-thoh

–IDO / EE-thoh for an **–ER** or **–IR** ending

tener--> ten**ido** / <u>t</u>eh-NEE-thoh

pedir--> ped**ido** / peh-THEE-thoh

Here are some past participles of verbs you have studied:

usado (from **usar**)	oo-SAH-thoh	used (past p.)
hablado (from **hablar**)	ah-BLAH-thoh	spoken (past p.)
comido (from **comer**)	coh-MEE-thoh	eaten (past. p.)
leído (from **leer**)	lay-EE-thoh	read (past p.)
ido (from **ir**)	EE-thoh	gone (past p.)

Check for Understanding

Been There, Done That. Turn the following infinitives into past participles. The –AR endings change to –ADO and the –ER and –IR endings change to –IDO. Answers are in the supplemental section.

1) beber (to drink)

2) ocupar (to occupy)

3) estar (to be—location, condition)

4) tener (to have, hold, keep)

5) leer (to read)

6) pedir (to ask for)

7) tomar (to take)

8) ser (to be—name, definition)

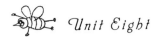

Special past participles

English has many irregular past participles, such as **gone**, **done**, **been**, **put**. In Spanish, there are very few irregulars.

A few rule-breakers that you should learn now are:

hecho (from **hacer**)	EH-choh	done, made (past p.)
puesto (from **poner**)	PWEHS-<u>t</u>oh	put (past p.)
escrito (from **escribir**)	eh-sk'DDEE-<u>t</u>oh	written (past p.)

NOTE: Compared to English, Spanish has relatively few irregular past participles. See "Been There, Done That" in the supplemental section for other common exceptions.

Using the past participle

Becoming familiar with the past participle and its related forms is a good way build your vocabulary and deepen your understanding of the different rules that apply to verbs, adjectives, and nouns in Spanish.

For example, past participles used as verbs always end in –O because Spanish verbs don't have gender. However, adjectives made from past participles do change endings, because adjectives must match the nouns they describe. Nouns derived from past participles don't change endings to match anything (changing the ending of a noun changes its meaning), but you do add –S to a noun to make it plural.

At first, concentrate on learning the meanings of the past participles that you will use most often. Once you know the meanings well, it will be easier to learn how and when you need to change their endings.

Check for Understanding

Practicing Past Participles. Practice turning other infinitives into past participles. Be careful of pronunciation. See "Been There, Done That" in the supplemental section for a list of irregular forms. If you want to make past participles for specialty verbs, use the following chart.

PAST PARTICIPLES IN YOUR SPECIALTY AREA (optional)

You can use adjectives derived from past participles to talk about the STATE of things or people in your specialty area. For example, you may need to say **El baño <u>está</u> ocupado** (The bathroom is occupied) or **El señor <u>está</u> lastimado** (The gentleman is injured).

You can also use the past participle to talk about events that have (or have not) happened. For example, you can say **La oficina <u>ha</u> cerrado** (The office has closed) or **La señora no <u>ha</u> regresado** (The lady has not returned).

Refer to, or make up, a list of the past participles that are most useful to your specialty area, using the verbs from Lesson Eleven. Make up a pronunciation guide using the chart at the beginning of Unit One. Then fill out this blank chart with the most important words. You may also wish to make flashcards.

SPANISH	PRONUNCIATION	ENGLISH

Recommended Practice for Beginners

Beginners should skip the following sections and go directly to the Lesson Sixteen expressions and mini-dialogues on page 8-23. You can come back later to read more about past participles as verbs, adjectives, and nouns.

C) BEEN THERE, DONE THAT: -ADO / -IDO with a VERB

One use of the **-ADO / -IDO** ending is to talk about things that have happened in the past.

There are several ways to talk about action in the past. For example, in English, to talk about "speaking" in the past, you can say "I spoke," "I used to speak," "I was speaking," and "I have spoken."

In Spanish, the <u>easiest</u> way for you to express actions that happened in the past is in the form "I have spoken." To express this form, you need to use the verb "to have done" something. It is different from **tengo, tiene, tienen**, which is "to have, hold, keep" something physical.

HAVE "DONE"

he	eh (close to letter "A")	I have (*-ed /-en)
ha	ah	You have, s/he has (*-ed /-en)
han	ahn	You all, they have (*-ed /-en)

(*-ed /-en) stands for the past participle of the verb: **used, spoken, written, gone**, etc.

The verbs **he** / eh, **ha** /ah, and **han** / ahn are used with a past participle to talk about something that you **have done** at some time in the past: "I have spoken," "You have watched," "He has returned," "They have done," etc.

He hablado.	I have spoken.
Ha mirado.	You or s/he have looked at.
Han comido.	You all or they have eaten.

NOTE: The word **ha** / ah can mean "You <u>have</u>," or "s/he <u>has</u>" done something, and the word **han** / ahn can mean "You all have" or "they have" done something.

It is <u>very</u> important to pronounce these words correctly, so be sure to follow the pronunciation guide. If you find yourself saying "he" and "ha" as in English, don't look at the Spanish spellings. Look at the guide.

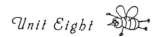

You can make sentences with **he** /eh, **ha** /ah, **han** /ahn and a past participle, using words and expressions from previous lessons.

¿Ha tomado la clase?	Have You taken the class?
Ya han ido a la junta.	They have already gone to the meeting.
He puesto la pluma allá.	I have put the pen over there.

As with other verbs you have learned, to make the verb negative, you put "no" in front of the verb.

No he hecho nada.	I haven't done "nothing."
No ha regresado.	S/he has not returned.

The infinitives that end in –RSE are more complicated, because the pronoun (me, se, etc.) breaks off and goes in front of the verb. If the sentence is negative, the "no" goes in front of everything. Refer to this example (from the verb **sentarse**, "to sit down"), if you must use an –RSE verb.

Me he sentado.	I have sat down.
No me he sentado.	I have not sat down.
Se ha sentado.	You, s/he have sat down.
No se ha sentado.	You, s/he have not sat down.

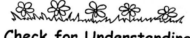

Check for Understanding

Have / Have Not Done. Make a study list or flashcards and practice the verbs in section C). Follow the steps outlined in "How to Practice Vocabulary" in Lesson Two. Then translate the following sentences into Spanish. Answers are in the supplemental section.

NOTE: The "no" in a negative sentence goes before **he, ha, han.** Also, you don't need to translate the words for "I," "he," "she," or "they."

1) Your dad has returned.

2) They have drunk water (**agua**).

3) Have You written to your mom?

4) I haven't looked at this (**esto**).

5) I have not done "nothing."

6) She has not gone to the office.

NOTES about -ADO and -IDO in the Past

When used as part of a <u>verb</u>, the past participle <u>always</u> ends in -O. It never changes ending. The only thing that changes is **he** / eh, **ha** /ah, or **han** / ahn.

The verbs **tengo, tiene, tienen** mean to physically "have," "hold," or "keep." To talk about things that <u>have happened</u> in the past, you will use **he** / eh, **ha** / ah, or **han** / ahn.

Because the past participles are mostly regular, you can start saying things in the past right away, without having to learn a lot of exceptions.

D) DESCRIBING: -ADO /-IDO (-ADA /-IDA) with ADJECTIVES

The -ADO / -IDO endings are also used quite frequently to describe people and things, in which case they are being used as **adjectives**.

In Lesson Three, you learned how to describe things using a functional word and a describing <u>noun</u> (in Spanish, for children, at work). Unlike nouns, <u>adjectives</u> describe a noun <u>directly</u>. Here are some past participle adjectives.

hecho	EH-choh	done, made (adj.)
usado	oo-SAH-thoh	used (adj.)
terminado	tai<u>rr</u>-mee-NAH-thoh	finished (adj.)
cansado	cahn-SAH-thoh	tired (adj.)
lastimado	lah-s<u>t</u>ee-MAH-thoh	hurt, injured (adj.)
ocupado	oh-koo-PAH-thoh	busy, occupied (adj.)

Words like "busy" and "tired" indicate a STATE of something (not its name or defining properties). Remember, if you want to describe the STATE of something, you use **está / están**. Look at these examples:

El niño <u>está</u> lastimado.
Los empleados <u>están</u> cansados.
La sopa <u>está</u> hecha.
Las mesas <u>están</u> ocupadas.

The child <u>is</u> hurt.
The employees <u>are</u> tired.
The soup <u>is</u> done.
The tables <u>are</u> occupied /busy.

Noun-Adjective Agreement

Spanish adjectives change their endings to match the nouns they describe. When you read or hear people speaking, you will notice that the endings of adjectives change.

For now, concentrate on learning the meanings of the adjectives. Once you know the meanings well, it will be easier to learn how to change their endings.

For more information on how to use adjectives, see the supplemental section.

Check for Understanding

Verb or Adjective? Translate to English. Notice the Spanish endings.

1) Papá está ocupado.

2) Mamá está ocupada.

3) El baño está ocupado.

4) La mesas están ocupadas.

5) Papá ha ocupado la mesa.

6) Mamá ha ocupado la mesa.

As you can see, the –O ending changes to -A to describe a female or feminine object, and you add an –S to describe something plural.

However, when you use -ADO, -IDO forms after **he** /eh, **ha** / ah, and **han** / ahn, to talk about the past, the ending is always -O.

Adjectives change endings to match gender, but verbs do not. Spanish verbs never have gender.

E) NAMING: -ADA / -IDA & -ADO / -IDO with NOUNS

So far you have learned to recognize the **-ADO / -IDO** endings in the past participle of the <u>verb</u> and in <u>adjectives</u>.

In Spanish, it is also common for <u>nouns</u> derived from verbs to end in **-ADA /** AH-thah and **-IDA /** EE-thah. (It is less common to see nouns ending in **-ADO /** AH-thoh and **-IDO /** EE-thoh, but it does happen.)

Look at these examples:

comer	coh-MAI*RR*	to eat
comida	coh-MEE-thah	food
beber	beh-BAI*RR*	to drink
bebida	beh-BEE-thah	beverage
entrar	ehn-*t*'ddAH*RR*	to enter
entrada	ehn-*t*'ddAH-thah	entrance
salir	sah-LEE*RR*	to exit, leave a place
salida	sah-LEE-thah	exit (n.)
llamar	yah-MAH*RR*	to call
llamada	yah-MAH-thah	telephone call

Please note that although it is quite common, the **-ADA / -IDA** ending won't turn all verbs into nouns, and not all nouns end in **-ADA / -IDA**.

Here are some examples of other noun endings:

reservar	*rr* eh-sai*rr*-VAH*RR*	to reserve
reservación (f.)	*rr* eh-sai*rr*-vah-s'YOHN	reservation
trabajar	*t*'ddah-bah-HAH*RR*	to work
trabajo	*t*'ddah-BAH-hoh	job, work, project
trabajador (m.)	*t*'ddah-bah-hah-THOH*RR*	worker, hard-working
comer	coh-MAI*RR*	to eat
comedor (m.)	coh-meh-THOH*RR*	dining hall
comestibles (m. pl.)	coh-meh-S<u>T</u>EE-blehss	groceries

Final Notes

You will know if a Spanish past participle is a verb, adjective or noun by how it is used in a sentence. For example, look at these sentences, which all use forms of **hecho** / EH-choh (done, made).

¿Ha hecho la sopa?   Have you made the soup? **(Expresses action: VERB)**
La sopa está hecha.   The soup is done. **(Describes a thing: ADJECTIVE)**
Es un hecho.   It's a fact. **(Names a thing: NOUN)**

Check for Understanding

Reserve. Translate to English. Notice the different endings and uses of the words that come from the verb **reservar** / *rr* eh-sai*rr*-VAH*RR* (to reserve).

1) Tengo una reservación.   3) Quiero reservar una mesa.

2) He reservado la mesa.   4) La mesa está reservada.

Lesson Sixteen Expressions

ya	yah	already
todavía no	t̲oh-thah-VEE-ah NOH	not yet
nunca	NOONG-cah	never
cansado	cahn-SAH-thoh	tired (m.)
cansada	cahn-SAH-thah	tired (f.)
lastimado	lah-s̲t̲ee-MAH-thoh	injured (m.)
lastimada	lah-s̲t̲ee-MAH-thah	injured (f.)
ocupado	oh-koo-PAH-thoh	busy, occupied (m.)
ocupada	oh-koo-PAH-thah	busy, occupied (f.)
Hasta luego	AH-s̲tah LWEH-goh	So long, see you later
Adiós	ah-th'YOHSS	Good-bye
Buena suerte	BWEH-nah SWAI*RR*-t̲eh	Good luck

Speaking Practice

Practice the Lesson Sixteen mini-dialogues. Work with a partner, if possible.
1) Each of the three dialogues practices a different use of the past participle (as verb, as adjective, and as noun). Be <u>very</u> sure to pronounce the "d" in the past participle as the "th" as in "brother."
2) In dialogue A, put a past participle in the blank, using the list. The ending of the past participle will always be –O because it is being used as a verb. Sometimes it will sound better to say "this" after the verb: "Have you read <u>this</u>?", and sometimes it will sound better without it: "Have you eaten (-)?"

Speaking Activities

1) Pick a dialogue and act it out. Work with a partner, and use props, if possible.
2) Write a dialogue based on the Lesson Sixteen mini-dialogues, and use ONLY the vocabulary presented in this lesson and previous lessons.
3) Act out your own dialogue. Work with a partner, and use props, if possible.

More Practice

1) Practice saying the Lesson Sixteen structures and expressions aloud, using the pronunciation guide. Work with a partner if you can.
2) Begin learning the Lesson Sixteen structures and expressions by heart. Make flashcards or a study list. Practice any specialty vocabulary.
3) Visit **www.spanishthatworks.org** for additional practice materials.

EXTRA: You can use the following words to describe <u>when</u> something is happening. For more information about how to recognize verbs in other tenses, see the supplemental section.

More Words to Describe When

hoy	OY	today
mañana	mahn-YAH-nah	tomorrow (also: morning)
ayer	ah-YAI*RR*	yesterday
entonces	ehn-<u>T</u>OHN-sehss	then
antes	AHN-<u>t</u>ehss	before
después	theh-SPWEHss	afterwards

Lesson Sixteen Mini-Dialogues:
Building Vocabulary

A) Past participles as action words

1) ¿Ya ha **(yah-ah)** _____ (esto)?	1) Have You already "<u>done</u>" (this)?
2) Sí, ya. He **(eh)** _____ (eso) en la mañana.	2) Yes, (already). I've "<u>done</u>" (that) in the morning.
OR	
2) No, todavía no. No he **(noh-eh)** _____ (nada / nunca).	2) No, not yet. I haven't "<u>done</u>" (nothing / never).

PAST PARTICIPLES ("DONE"):   *(Use "th" for the "d"!)*
leído, escrito, tomado, usado, mirado, regresado, ido, preparado, comido, OTHER

B) Using past participles to describe people

1) ¿Cómo está su (amigo / hijo / esposo / papá / colega / trabajo)?	1) How is Your (friend / son / husband / dad / co-worker / job)?
2) Pues, está (cansado / lastimado / ocupado / bien).	2) Well, he's (tired / injured / busy / fine).
1) ¿Cómo está su (amiga / hija / esposa / mamá / colega / familia)?	1) How is Your (friend / daughter / wife / mom / co-worker / family)?
2) Pues, está (cansada / lastimada / ocupada / bien).	2) Well, she's (tired / injured / busy / fine).

C) Nouns derived from past participles

1) Perdón, ¿dónde está (la comida / la bebida / la entrada / la salida)?	1) Excuse me, where is (the food / the beverage / the entrance / the exit)?
2) Pues, allá, mire. *Points.*	2) Well, over there, see. *Points.*
1) Gracias. Adiós, hasta luego.	1) Thanks. Good-bye, so long.
2) ¡Adiós y buena suerte!	2) Good-bye and good luck!

EXTRA NOTE:

Many Spanish nouns and adjectives are formed by adding a suffix to the end of a root word. Usually the root word and the new word are related.

For example, **libro** means "book," while **librería** means "bookstore." **Trabajo** means "job," while **trabajador** means "worker."

By focusing on the root of a word, you can often deduce the word's meaning within the context of the sentence.

Bee Bilingual!

SUPPLEMENTAL SECTION:

"You speak Spanish very well!"

More Information

ABOUT THE SUPPLEMENTAL SECTION

The supplemental section includes more detailed explanations of some of the concepts presented in *Spanish that Works for You*, as well as extra information not directly covered in the course text. Students can refer to this section on their own as needed and instructors can use it to extend the course curriculum beyond the basic eight units.

At the end of this section is the answer key to the "Check for Understanding" exercises. The purpose of the exercises is to make sure that the students understand the concepts presented in the text.

Additional materials (many for free) are available at **www.spanishthatworks.org (www.thelearninglight.com)**. These include a teacher's guide, pull-out reference sheets, and cut-out flashcard pages.

Also available via the website are: an audio program with the basic vocabulary covered in the course, a distance-learning video series of the course done live-to-tape for community television, specialty vocabulary modules, supplemental lessons, other instructor resources, and recommendations for further study.

GUIDELINES FOR LEARNING ON YOUR OWN

The following suggestions are for all students, but are especially important for those individuals working through *Spanish that Works for You* on their own.

Structure your Studies

Create a regular practice time to review the course text and materials such as flashcards or pull-out reference sheets. If you are working on your own, set up a specific time to go over the lessons, as if you were taking a real class.

Get a study partner. The idea is to learn how to interact verbally with other people, so it is better if you can talk with someone else. If you set an appointment to meet with a study partner, you are more likely to stay on task.

Write out the answers to the "Check for Understanding" activities on a separate piece of paper, so you can go back later on and quiz yourself again. If you create specialty vocabulary lists, have a Spanish speaker check your work.

Work on your Pronunciation

Read Lesson One thoroughly, even if you think you already know how to pronounce Spanish. The pronunciation guide that is used in this course was designed to help English speakers approximate the sounds of Spanish more closely.

Listen to the audio program or have someone with native or near-native pronunciation of Spanish pronounce the words in the text for you. Then, have the Spanish speaker listen to you pronounce the core vocabulary words and correct you on any troublesome sounds. Good pronunciation is the foundation for understanding and being understood, so it is essential that you get proper feedback.

The pronunciation guide does not make sense to non-native English speakers, so don't expect Spanish speakers to understand it. Just read the guide as an English nonsense word, and trust that it will work. If you are NOT a native speaker of English, you may have to make some adjustments to the guide, especially for the R and D.

Create a Practice Group

Consider the possibility of organizing a *Spanish that Works* class or follow-up practice group in your workplace or community. The method and materials are simple and teacher orientation materials and training are available, so even Spanish speakers who are not professional language teachers can successfully use these materials to lead your group.

Immerse Yourself in the Language

Get some music in Spanish to train your ear to the language. Read the lyrics as you listen along, to reinforce correct pronunciation of the letters. You can find many different types of music at your local library or bookstore. For links to recommended music CD's, visit our website: **www.spanishthatworks.org.**

Watch television or movies in Spanish. Listen for the words you know, and see what you can pick up from context clues and body language.

Seek out situations where you will be around Spanish speakers. There are probably people in your community who speak Spanish, so you don't necessarily need to travel. But, by all means travel if you can. It's fun!

BEE BILINGUAL!

After you complete the course, let us know via email what worked, what could have helped you better, and what you would like to see next, so that we can continue to improve and expand on *Spanish that Works*.

Have faith and have fun. You can do it!

Elizabeth Almann, author
The Learning Light, LLC
Educational Materials & Service
info@thelearninglight.com

LEARNING NEW VOCABULARY

Spanish that Works gives you a good practical knowledge of conversational Spanish, as well as a solid foundation for further study of Spanish grammar. You will want to master what you learn in this course, but you will also want to be able to learn new material and integrate it into what you know.

Keep these recommendations in mind as you learn new vocabulary.

1) Rehearse Vocabulary in Steps

When you study your flashcards or vocabulary lists, you should follow these steps, which are introduced in Unit One (Lesson Two).

Rehearsing: Saying & Learning. Read the Spanish words aloud, paying attention to correct pronunciation. After you say the word, look at its meaning (English word). Do this until you are familiar with the meanings of the words.

Think up a visual cue, sound-alike word, or other word association to jog your memory. For example, to recall the Spanish word for pen, you might visualize using a feather plume, as in an old-fashioned quill pen. Pen—plume—**pluma**.

If you are having difficulty pronouncing the words when you look at the Spanish spellings, use ONLY the pronunciation guide. This is a conversation course, so the sound is more important than the spelling.

Quiz: Understanding the Spanish. Quiz yourself with flashcards or the word list by reading the Spanish side with the English side covered. Check yourself after each word. If you don't know one, put it aside. Practice the ones you didn't know, using memory devices.

Quiz: Saying the Spanish. Quiz yourself with flashcards or the word list by reading the English side with the Spanish side covered. Check yourself after each word. If you don't know one, put it aside. Practice the ones you didn't know, using memory devices.

After you know the words, keep quizzing yourself to improve your pronunciation and speed of recall. You may skip the rehearsing step when you are reviewing.

2) Pay Attention to Endings

Learn the words in your lessons exactly, with particular attention to word ending. For example, "Good morning" is **Buenos días** (note the –O in **buenos**), while "Good afternoon" is **Buenas tardes** (note the –A in **buenas**). This may not seem like much of a difference, but it is an example of noun-adjective agreement, which is an essential part of Spanish grammar. Many English speakers turn the –O in **buenos** into an –A sound. This is a grammar mistake, because **días** is masculine.

Native speakers may use words that are similar to ones you have been learning, but which have different endings. For example, you will learn the word **Mire** (Look!) and **mirar** (to look). There are many other endings for this verb, including **miro** (I look), **mira** (You, s/he look), and **miran** (You all, they look). For now, see if you can notice any patterns in the endings of the words you are studying, and learn the basic vocabulary thoroughly and accurately. You may not understand exactly why an ending is the way it is, but if you learn it correctly, you will create a good foundation for future study of the language.

3) Know the Part of Speech

When you learn words beyond this course, it is very important to know **the part of speech** (noun, verb, adjective, etc.), which will indicate how the word is to be used in a sentence. For example, if you look up "can" in the dictionary, you will get the noun "can" (**lata, n.**: a cylindrical object made of tin used for food) and the verb "can" (**poder, v.**: to be able to).

If you do not pay attention to the part of speech (and the usage, for words which have multiple meanings), you may end up with sentences that make no sense at all. For example:

Yo <u>lata</u> ir.   I <u>tin can for food</u> go.
Quiero un <u>poder</u> de vegetales.   I want a <u>to be able to</u> of vegetables.

Which makes no sense! What you want to say is:

<u>Puedo</u> participar.   I <u>can (am able to)</u> participate.
Quiero una <u>lata</u> de vegetales.   I want a <u>tin can</u> of vegetables.

THE PARTS OF SPEECH

"Part of speech" means how the word is used in a sentence.

noun (n.) A noun is a thing, person, place, or idea. It is something you can have, or someone or something that can do something. You will learn many practical nouns in this course, which include names of things, places, and people. Spanish nouns have **gender** (masculine / feminine) and **number** (singular / plural).

pronoun (p.n.) or (pron.) A pronoun takes the place of a noun. Subject pronouns (I, you, he, she, etc.) are not required in Spanish. The only subject pronouns you will use in this course are **usted** (You) and **ustedes** (You all).

verb (v.) A verb expresses an action or a state of being. It is something you do or are. Spanish verbs show **person** (I, You, etc.), and **tense** (time of action). You will learn a few essential verbs such as **necesito** (I need) and **quiere** (You want), as well as some infinitives, such as **mirar** (to look at).

adjective (adj.) An adjective describes a noun directly. Spanish adjectives change form to agree with, or match, a noun (masculine / feminine and singular / plural). You will not use many descriptive adjectives in this course. However, you will learn the possessive adjectives **mi** (my) and **su** (Your). You will also indirectly learn the adjective **bueno** (good).

adverb (adv.) An adverb usually describes a verb (action or state of being). Some adverbs you will use in the course are **no** (no or not), and **bien** (fine, well).

Sometimes an adverb describes an adjective or another adverb. You will learn the adverb **muy** (very), which can describe the adjective "good": **muy bueno** (very good) or the adverb "well": **muy bien** (very well).

preposition (prep.) A preposition is a functional word that establishes relationships between other words in the sentence. Prepositions don't usually translate word for word between languages. Some prepositions you will learn include **para** (intended for), **por** (for receipt of, per), and **de** (of, from).

conjunction (conj.) A conjunction also establishes relationship in a sentence. Conjunctions you will learn include **y** (and) and **o** (or).

MORE ABOUT VOCABULARY

Variety in Spanish

There is often more than one correct way to say something in a language. Sometimes choice of word depends on one's country or area of origin, and sometimes it is a manner of personal preference.

This is common in English. For example, that which a person from the U.S. would call a **truck,** in Britain is referred to as a **lorry.** Even within the United States there is variety. People may refer to soft drinks as **soda, pop,** or **coke,** depending on where they come from, or where they live.

There is diversity in Spanish, too. A speaker from Mexico might say **pluma** for a ballpoint pen, while a Spaniard would use the word **bolígrafo.** The expressions **¡Claro!, ¡Por supuesto!** and **¡Cómo no!** can all be used to mean **Of course!** A car may be referred to as a **coche, carro, auto,** or **automóvil,** depending on the origin of the speaker.

In these examples, although there is variety among the vocabulary words, all are considered to be "standard" Spanish. A Spanish speaker might use **coche** or **carro,** but would understand both.

The words and expressions taught in *Spanish that Works* should be accepted as standard language by most educated Latin American speakers. Some speakers may prefer to use other vocabulary (or spelling), but they should understand the terms you are studying.

It is best to use standard terms whenever possible. For one thing, regional variations may not be understood by all Spanish speakers. You cannot assume to know the background or level of education of everyone you meet, so you want to use the words that are most likely to be universally understood.

Using standard language also conveys competence and authority. It is not a question of being "right" or "wrong," but rather one of image. If you use standard language, you will be understood by the majority and you will also make a good impression.

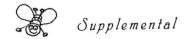

THE SPANISH ALPHABET

Use the names of the letters if you need to spell something aloud.

LETTER	LETTER NAME	PRONUNCIATION
a	a	ah
b	be grande	beh g'DDAHN-theh
c	ce	seh
d	de	theh
e	e	eh
f	efe	EH-feh
g	ge	heh
h	hache	AH-cheh
i	i	ee
j	jota	HOH-tah
k	ka	kah
l	ele	EH-leh
m	eme	EH-meh
n	ene	EH-neh
ñ	eñe	EHN-yeh
o	o	oh
p	pe	peh
q	cu	coo
r	ere	EH-ddeh
rr	erre	EH-*rr*eh
s	ese	EH-sseh
t	te	teh
u	u	oo
v	ve chica	beh CHEE-cah
w	doble ve, doble u	THOH-bleh VEH /OO
x	equis	EH-kees
y	y griega	ee g'ddee-EH-gah
z	zeta	SEH-tah

1. Since the b and v sound the same in Spanish, native speakers will specify the "big" b *(b grande)* or the "little" v *(v chica)*. Some speakers say *be de burro* (b in *burro*, which means *donkey*), and *ve de vaca* (v in *vaca*, which means *cow*).
2. When you spell a Spanish word with an accent mark, you say the vowel first, and then the word *acento* (ah-SEHN-toh). Example: **aquí:** *A-cu-u-i, acento.*
3. The **ch** (**che** / CHEH) and **ll** (**elle** / EH-yeh) used to be considered separate letters in Spanish. This has changed.

SOCIAL LANGUAGE

From the "Basic Customer Service" Reference Sheet

The following words and expressions are used throughout *Spanish that Works for You,* and will be very helpful to you as you learn Spanish.

All of the words except those marked "Extra" are organized on a "Basic Customer Service" reference sheet (see **www.spanishthatworks.org**) and are covered on the audio program.

Greetings, etc.

Buenos días / BWEH-nohss THEE-ahss / Good morning (Hello)
Buenas tardes / BWEH-nahss TAH*RR*-thehss /
Good afternoon, evening (Hello)
Buenas noches / BWEH-nahss NOH-chess / Good night

¿En qué puedo servirle? / ehn keh PWEH-thoh sai*rr*-VEE*RR*-leh? /
How may I help You?

¿Qué necesita? / KEH neh-seh-SEE-tah? / What do You need?

¿Necesita ayuda? / neh-seh-SEE-tah ah-YOO-thah? /
Do You need help? (polite)

¿Me da...? / meh THAH...? / Will You give me (Can I have)?
Extra: **¿Me trae...?** / meh t'ddAH-ey (vowel like "try")...? / Will You bring me?

Hasta luego / AH-stah LWEH-goh / So long, until later

Adiós / ah-th'YOHss / Good-bye

¿Aló? / ah-LOH? / Hello? (phone)

¿Bueno? / BWEH-noh? / Hello? (phone, Mexico)

Courtesy

Por favor. / POH*RR* fah-VOH*RR* / Please.

Gracias. / g'DDAH-s'yahss / Thanks.

De nada. / theh NAH-thah / You're welcome.

Lo siento. / loh S'YEHN-<u>t</u>oh / I'm sorry.

Perdón. / pai*rr*-THOHN / Excuse me.
Extra: Disculpe. / thees-COOL-peh / Excuse me.

Está bien. / eh-S<u>T</u>AH b'YEHN / It's fine.

Ah, bueno. / ah BWEH-noh / Oh, okay, good.

¡Claro! / CLAHddoh! / Of course! (Clearly)
Extra: ¡Cómo no! / COH-moh noh! / Of course (How not?)

No hay problema. / noh-AYE p'ddoh-BLEH-mah / (There's) no problem.

Negotiating Meaning

No entiendo. / noh ehn <u>T</u>'YEHN-thoh / I don't understand.

¿Entiende? / ehn-<u>T</u>'YEHN-theh? / Do You understand?

¿Cómo se dice? / KOH-moh seh THEE-seh? / How does one say...?

Repita, por favor. / *rr*eh-PEE-tah, POH*RR* fah-VOH*RR* / Repeat, please.

Más despacio. / mahss theh-SPAH-s'yoh / More slowly.

¿Cómo? / COH-moh? / What? (How did you say it)?

No sé. / noh-SAY / I don't know.

No hablo (mucho) español. / noh AH-bloh (MOOchoh) eh-spahn-YOHL /
I don't speak (much) Spanish.

¿Habla inglés? / AH-blah een-GLEHSS? / Do you speak English?

Un momento. / oon moh-MEHN-toh / One moment.

Mi colega habla español. / mee coh-LEH-gah AH-blah eh-spahn-YOHL /
My co-worker speaks Spanish.

Sólo un poco (un poquito). / SOH-loh oon POH-coh (oon poh-KEE-toh) /
Only a little bit (a tiny little bit)

Pues... / PWEHss / So... then...

Eso es. / EH-soh ehss / That's it.

¿no? / NOH? / right?
Used to ask if a statement is correct,
such as "It's your book, right?"(**Es su libro, ¿no?**)

---

sí / see / yes
no / noh / no
(**No** also means "not" or "don't" when used before a verb)

mi / mee / my
(When more than one thing is being possessed, you say **mis** / mees)

su / soo / Your (can also mean his, her, its, or their)
(When more than one thing is being possessed, you say **sus** / soos)

aquí / ah-KEE / here

allá / ah-YAH / over there

For more strategies that you can use to negotiate meaning,
refer to Unit Five (Lesson Ten).

Questions

¿Cuál es su… / KWAHL-ehss soo… / What (which) is Your…

nombre? / NOHM-b'ddeh? / name?

número? / NOO-meh-ddoh? / number?

dirección? thee-ddehk-s'YOHN? / address?

edad? / eh-THAth? / age?

¿Cuál es el problema? / KWAHL-ehss ehl p'ddoh-BLEH-mah? /
What (which) is the problem?

¿Qué es? / kay-EHSS? / What is (it)? (definition)

¿Cuándo es? / KWAHN-thoh-EHSS? / When is (it)?

¿Dónde está? / THOHN-theh-eh-S̲TAH? / Where is it, s/he, You?

¿Dónde están? / THOHN-theh-eh-S̲TAHN? / Where are they, You all?

¿Cómo está? / KOH-moh eh-S̲TAH? / How are You / How is it?

¿Cuánto es? / KWAHN-toh ehss? / How much is it?

EXTRA: ¿Cuántos? / KWAHN-tohss / How many? (m. pl.)
¿Cuántas? / KWAHN-tahss / How many? (f. pl.)

¿Por cuánto tiempo? / poh*rr* KWAHN-toh t̲'YEHM-poh? / For how long?

¿Quién es? / k'YEHN ehss / Who is it?

¿Para quién es? / PAHddah k'YEHN ehss? / Who is it for? (For whom is it?)

Commands

Espere. / eh-SPEH-ddeh / Wait.

Pase. / PAH-seh / Come in.

Escriba. / eh-sk'DEE-bah / Write.

Lea. / LAY-ah / Read.

Mire. / MEE-ddeh / Look.

Extra: **Escuche.** / eh-SKOO-cheh / Listen.

Formula Commands

Favor de (no) + <u>infinitive</u>. / fah-VOH*RR* theh (noh) + <u>infinitive</u> /
Please (don't) + <u>infinitive</u>.

An infinitive is the form of the verb that you would find if you looked the verb up in the dictionary. Spanish infinitives in the dictionary end in –R or –RSE. For more information, see Unit Six (Lessons Eleven and Twelve).

¿Necesita ayuda?
Do you need help?

Es usted muy amable.
You're very kind.

MORE ABOUT SOCIAL LANGUAGE

Saying "Hello"

The word **hola** / OH-lah, looks like "hello," but it is actually closer to "hi." You could use **hola** to greet a friend, but you probably would not want to use **hola** to greet someone you did not know.

With strangers, customers, storekeepers, and others with whom you maintain a professional distance, it is better to use **Buenos días** / BWEH-nohss THEE-ahss (Good day) and **Buenas tardes** / BWEH-nahss <u>T</u>AH*RR*-thehss (Good afternoon). After dark, you can use **Buenas noches** / BWEH-nahss NOH-chess (Good night).

Also, most speakers don't use **hola** on the phone. To answer the phone, say **¿Aló?** / ah-LOH? (Latin America) or **¿Bueno?** / BWEH-noh? (Mexico only).

The **hola** by itself is casual, but you can use it to make **Buenos días** and **Buenas tardes** sound friendlier. So, **Hola, buenos días** and **Hola, buenas tardes**, are still polite and respectful, but a little more personal.

Good-byes

The expression **adiós** / ah-th'YOHSS (good-bye) is used when you are not expecting to see someone for awhile. You can also use **adiós** to end a phone conversation.

If you are going to be seeing someone again soon, use the expression **hasta luego** / ah-s<u>t</u>ah LWEH-goh (until later, see you later). If you will see the person the next day, say **hasta mañana** / AH-s<u>t</u>ah mahn-YAH-nah (until tomorrow, see you tomorrow).

Sometimes speakers will combine these expressions, to say **adiós, hasta luego,** or **adiós, hasta mañana,** etc.

The expression **hasta la vista** (so long, see you later) is cute, but a bit on the slang side, so it's better to use the more standard phrase **hasta luego.**

Common Courtesy

Just as in English, it always helps to say **por favor** / POHRR fah-VOHRR (please), **gracias** / g'DDAH-s'yahss (thanks) and **de nada** / theh NAH-thah (you're welcome).

The expression **de nada** literally means "of nothing." Some other ways to say "You're welcome" are: **es un placer** / eh-soon-plah-SAIRR (it's a pleasure) and **gracias a** <u>usted</u> / g'DDAH-s'yahss ah oo-STETH (thank <u>you</u>.)

Please note that in Spanish you say **por favor** (please) when requesting something, and **gracias** (thanks) when accepting something. In English, when someone asks if you want something, you say "Yes, please." But in Spanish, if someone offers you something, you say **Sí, gracias** (Yes, thanks) to accept.

However, if you want someone to give you something, and you need to ask for it, you say **por favor** (please) to request the item.

To express gratitude for helpful service, Spanish speakers often use the expression **Es usted muy amable** / ehss-oo-STETH mooy ah-MAH-bleh (You're very kind).

And, of course, you don't have to greet strangers as if they were your close friends, but a pleasant, helpful expression goes a long way in letting people know that you are willing to work with them. It takes a long time to become completely fluent in a language, but it only takes a few seconds to smile.

Meeting People

The easiest way to introduce yourself to someone is to say, **Hola, buenos días, soy...** (Hello, I'm...) and then give your name.

The polite response to an introduction is **Mucho gusto** / MOO-choh GOO-stoh (Much pleasure, nice to meet you).

The polite response to **Mucho gusto** is **El gusto es mío** / ehl GOO-stoh ehss MEE-oh (The pleasure is mine). You can also say **Igualmente** / ee-gwahl-MEHN-teh (Same to you, nice to meet you also).

Inquiring about Someone's Health

In the United States, it is common to use "How are you?" as a greeting, rather than as an expression of concern about the state of someone's health or well being. You casually say "How are you?" as you walk by, and sometimes you don't even hear the answer.

Be aware that if you ask a Spanish speaker **¿Cómo está?** (How are You?), you should wait for a response. Otherwise, you might seem uncaring.

If you don't really care how the person is, and just want to be friendly, stick with **Hola, buenos días** and **Hola, buenas tardes.**

Just so you know, the polite way to respond to **¿Cómo está?** (How are You?) is **Bien, gracias. ¿Y usted?** / b'YEHN g'DDAH-s'yahss, ee oo-STETH? (Fine, thanks. And You?)

The way to say "How nice!" is **¡Qué bueno!** / keh BWEH-noh!

Titles

The words **señor** (Mr., Sir), **señora** (Mrs., Ma'am), and **señorita** (Miss), can be used alone, or with a last name. So, you can say **señor García, señora Villa,** and **señorita Flores**, if you know the last name. Otherwise, you can just say **señor, señora,** and **señorita.**

A boy can be addressed as **joven** (Young man) if you do not know his name, or as Mr. so-and-so (**señor ___**) if you do know his name. So, you could call a young man **señor Rodríguez,** but to get his attention, you might address him as **joven**. You could also say **señor.**

There is no Spanish equivalent for Ms., so a woman is either **señora** or **señorita**. Sometimes, older women are called **señora,** whether married or not. Women in customer service jobs are often addressed as **señorita,** regardless of their age.

Buenos días, señorita.
Good day, Miss.

NUMBERS ABOVE 100

Unit Seven (Lessons Thirteen and Fourteen) in *Spanish that Works for You* teaches the numbers 1—100, and how to say the time and the date. Below are the numbers 100 and above, for your reference.

The "Numbers, Time, Day, Date" reference sheet (**www.spanishthatworks.org**) organizes the numbers, days of the week, months of the year, how to give the time and the date, and the words for dollars and cents all on a single hand-out. There is also a "Numbers, Time, Day, Date" section on the audio program.

100   **cien** / s'YEHN
101   **ciento uno** / s'YEHN-toh OO-noh
158   **ciento cincuenta y ocho**
         s'YEHN-toh seen-KWEHN-tah ee OH-choh
200   **doscientos** / thoh-s'YEHN-tohss
220   **doscientos veinte**
         thoh-s'YEHN-tohss BANE-tay
300   **trescientos** / t'ddeh-s'YEHN-tohss
400   **cuatrocientos** / KWAH-t'ddoh s'YEHN-tohss
500   **quinientos** / keen-YEHN-tohss
600   **seiscientos** / sayce- s'YEHN-tohss
700   **setecientos** / SEH-teh s'YEHN-tohss
800   **ochocientos** / OH-choh- s'YEHN-tohss
900   **novecientos** / noh-veh s'YEHN-tohss

1000 **mil** / MEEL
1015 **mil quince** / MEEL KEEN-seh
1999 **mil novecientos noventa y nueve**
         MEEL noh-veh s'YEHN-tohss noh-VEHN-tah ee NWEH-veh

NOTE: Numbers in the thousands, including years, are expressed in Spanish as the complete number, and never in the form "nineteen (hundred) ninety-nine."

2000 **dos mil** / thohs MEEL
2001 **dos mil uno** / thohs meel OO-noh

1,000,000   **un millón** / oon mee-YOHN
40,000,000   **cuarenta millones** / kwah-ddEHN-tah mee-YOH-nehss

ABOUT SPANISH VERBS

Spanish verbs can be a challenge because they are conjugated, or change form to show **person** (I, you, he, she, etc.) and **tense**, (past, present, future, ongoing vs. completed action, etc.). Spanish verbs also have **command forms** and **mood** (indicative vs. subjunctive). A Spanish speaker may use a verb like **hablar** (to speak) in over 90 different constructions.

However, you don't need to know how to conjugate verbs in order to start speaking Spanish. In fact, thinking about the rules of the conjugation can be more of a hindrance than a help when you are trying to participate in a fast-moving conversation.

This does not mean that you can't learn a few verbs in their conjugated forms. When you study the verbs in your *Spanish that Works* lessons, you are learning conjugations. The difference is, you are learning the example, rather than the rule. You can use the example now, in conversation. Once you have practiced the example so much that it seems natural, you can use the example as a reference to start learning and applying the rules in other contexts.

Spanish that Works specifically limits the verbs and verb forms you study, so you can focus on simple, practical communication. First of all, you concentrate on three verb forms: **I, You, s/he**, and **You all, they** (Lesson Seven). Secondly, you learn how to use the present tense to express both the immediate future (Lesson Twelve) and the past (Lesson Sixteen). You learn how to make a two-part sentence using a verb such as "I want" and an infinitive such as "to speak" to construct sentences such as "I want to speak Spanish." Finally, you learn how to make commands using **Favor de (no)** and an infinitive (Lesson Eleven).

The following section explains more about the **tú** form ("buddy-buddy" you), the **vosotros** form (ye), and the **nosotros** form (we). It gives tips for understanding verbs in other tenses, and provides some supplemental verb vocabulary.

If you want to learn more about Spanish verb conjugations, any traditional grammar textbook will explain them to you in great detail. But remember, you don't need to know all the tenses to start communicating with someone today!

THE "BUDDY-BUDDY" YOU

Spanish that Works only teaches **usted** / oo STETH (and the plural **ustedes**), which is the polite way to say "You." Spanish also has a more intimate and informal "you," which speakers in Latin America and Mexico use with personal friends, subordinates, and children. You can think of the **tú** form as the "buddy-buddy you."

In order to use the polite **usted** form, you must use verbs that end in a vowel (or a vowel plus –N for the plural).

Look at these structures.

tiene	T͟YEH-neh	You have (polite, professional)
¿necesita?	neh-seh-SEE-t͟ah?	Do You need? (polite, professional)
¿Cómo está?	KOH-moh eh-S͟TAH?	How are You? (polite, professional)

In most tenses, including the present tense, the **tú** form has an –S at the end of the verb. Using this final –S is like being "buddy-buddy" with someone.

tienes	T͟YEH-nehss	you have (buddy-buddy)
¿necesitas?	neh-seh-SEE-t͟ahss?	Do you need? (buddy-buddy)
¿Cómo estás?	KOH-moh eh-S͟TAHSS?	How are you? (buddy-buddy)

Think of the –S at the end of the verb like saying "buddy" to the person.

Respect is extremely important in Latino culture. Even if you learned to use the "buddy" **tú** form at home with your family or in high school as a teenager, there are several advantages to using the polite **usted** form.

First of all, the word "buddy" is used here to describe the **tú** form instead of the traditional textbook description of "informal" because people in the U.S. are generally informal with everyone, including elders and strangers. However, in Latino culture, traditional forms of respect are still maintained.

Outside of the family, it is normally not appropriate to be buddy-buddy with anyone except a child or close friend. Some adults would view it as disrespectful or offensive to be called the buddy-buddy "you" (**tú**) by a younger person, a stranger, or someone in a professional capacity. Others might not take offense, but could interpret the buddy –S as a sign that you consider them to be a personal friend or romantic interest.

It is common in Mexico and Latin America for speakers to use **usted** with people they know quite well. Many children even use **usted** with their parents. Rather than being "formal," **usted** is a way to show respect.

Another advantage of using **usted** is that the verb forms are the same as for the third person singular (he and she form). The "buddy" –S ending confuses English speakers because in English, the –S goes on he/she verbs: **You have,** but **he or she ha**s. In Spanish, the –S goes on the "buddy-buddy" you: **tú tiene**s.

By using the **usted** form, you can think of the verb that ends in a vowel as being singular (You, s/he). So you say **usted tiene** (You have), **Margarita tiene** (Margarita has), and **el señor Gómez tiene** (Mr. Gomez has).

Although native speakers would normally use the **tú** form with a child, it is not incorrect to use the **usted** form. In fact, this polite distance is desirable if you want a child to behave. Native speakers often use **usted** to get children to pay attention, similar to using the complete name or a title in English (Miss Elizabeth Carol Thompson!)

Once you have complete fluency with the **usted** form, you can begin to add the –S when speaking to a child or a close personal friend. But in the beginning, it's best to keep it simple.

Polite Commands

The "buddy" **tú** command forms are harder to recognize, because the affirmative commands do not end in –S. For example, you may have heard Spanish speakers saying **Mira** / MEE-ddah, which is the **tú** command for "Look!" The polite, professional **usted** command is **Mire** / MEE-ddeh.

If you are not sure whether a command you have learned is intimate or polite, you can say **usted** after the command. This way, the person will know that you meant to be polite, even if you got the ending wrong. For example, if you added **usted** to the **tú** command **Mira**, and said **Mira usted**, the person would likely interpret the command as a polite request.

You can also make commands using the expressions **Favor de** / fah-VOHRR theh ("Please do") and **Favor de no** / fah-VOHRR theh noh ("Please don't), plus an infinitive verb. For more information about making commands using this formula, please see Lesson Eleven.

You vs. Your

Just as there are different words for **you** in Spanish, there are also different words for **your**.

The polite words for **You** and **Your** look very different from one another.

| usted (Ud.) | oo-STETH | You (professional, polite) |
| su / sus | soo / soos | Your (professional, polite) |

NOTES: *Spanish that Works* often uses a capital letter for "You' (**usted**) and "Your" (**su**) to remind you that you are using the polite, professional form of address. The word **su** (or **sus**, when a plural object is being possessed) can also translate as **his**, **her**, **their**, and **its**. However, in this course, you will mostly use **su / sus** to mean **Your**.

The "buddy-buddy" words for **you** and **your** sound exactly the same. However, the word for **you** is written with an accent mark.

| tú (note accent mark) | too | you (buddy-buddy) |
| tu / tus | too / toos | your (buddy-buddy) |

¿Quiere usted un lápiz?

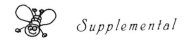

THE "YE" FORM ("BUDDY-BUDDY" YOU PLURAL)

In the Americas, the polite word **ustedes** (You all or You plural) and the –N ending on the verb (**tienen, están, necesitan**) are used with "buddy-buddy" groups, such as children and close friends, as well as with more polite contacts.

The true plural of the "buddy-buddy" **tú** form is **vosotros**. The vosotros form is only used in Spain, and sounds archaic to Latin Americans, much as the word **ye** sounds in English. The ending for vosotros is –**IS** (or –**D** for commands): **tenéis, estáis, mirad**. You will not learn any vosotros verbs in the basic course.

Do not confuse the word **vosotros** (ye) with **nosotros** (we).

THE "WE" FORM

In this course, the only "we" verb you will actively practice is **¡Vamos!** (Let's go!). **Vamos** is a good "we" verb to learn first because it can be used as a command.

For other verbs, the "we" form is long, and sometimes a little different from the "I" and "You" forms. In conversation, you can usually convey the same idea in a "we" verb (such as "we have") by using an "I" verb ("I have"), or a "s/he" verb ("the class has").

To achieve fluency in Spanish, you need to be able to recall things immediately. This is easier if you have fewer verbs to remember.

Although you won't be actively practicing "we" verbs, you can still learn to recognize them in speech. The verb ending for "we" in Spanish is <u>always</u> –**MOS**.

Examples:
> **necesitamos** (we need), **tenemos** (we have), **queremos** (we want),
> **hablamos** (we speak), **miramos** (we look), **entendemos** (we understand)

The word for "we" is **nosotros** / noh-SOH-t'ddohss, and the word for "our" (m.) is **nuestro** / NWEHSS-t'ddoh.

¡Vamos a hablar español!

RECOGNIZING VERBS IN OTHER TENSES

The verbs presented in *Spanish that Works* are all in the present tense. You only need the present tense (I want, you need, she speaks, etc.), to be able talk about past, present, and future in Spanish.

Spanish speakers often use the present tense to talk about the immediate future. For example, the verb "I speak" (**hablo** / AH-bloh), which is introduced in Lesson Ten, can mean "I do speak," "I am speaking," or even "I will speak." The verb "going to" (**voy, va, van**), which is covered in Lesson Twelve, can be used to talk about something you "will" do. You can talk about the past using the present perfect tense (I have done that, you have been there), which is covered in Lesson Sixteen.

However, you will hear native speakers using many different verb endings, depending on the tense, or time, of the action. There are endings for past, future, and what you "would" do. There are endings for commands and for talking about things that may or may not be.

You don't need to know all these endings right now, but it is helpful to know that they do exist. Most verbs are still recognizable in other tenses if you can identify the very beginning of the word.

For example, you will not learn the verb **miró**, but the beginning looks like **mire** (Look!), which is covered in Lesson Five. In fact, **miró** means **You, s/he looked**, in the past. (The I and You, s/he forms always end in a vowel (or vowel plus "y"), but the vowels change, depending on the tense.)

You can often guess <u>what</u> action is being talked about, even if you do not know <u>when</u> or <u>who</u>. If you hear a verb in context, such as "La clase miró un video," and use your imagination, you can deduce the meaning.

The plural –N (You all, they), and the –MOS (we) endings are consistent throughout ALL the tenses, so if something ends in –N or –MOS, you will also know <u>who</u>. You may also recognize the buddy –S which is on most of the intimate "you" or **tú** form verbs. And although you will not learn the **vosotros** ("ye") form, the endings are easy to spot: –IS or –D.

For now, if the verb ends in a vowel, all you will be able to tell is that the verb is singular. Sometimes it will be "I," sometimes "You, s/he" and sometimes all of these. For example, the verb **hablo** / AH-bloh is an "I" verb (I speak), but the verb **habló** / ah-BLOH is a "You, s/he" verb (You, s/he spoke). The verb **hablaría** / ah-blah-DDEE-ah means "I, You, he, or she would speak." In the simple past tense, even the **tú** form verbs end in a vowel (for example: **hablaste** / ah-BLAH-s̲teh, which means "you spoke").

In a compound verb such as **he tomado** (I have taken), the "Who" is in the first word, **he** /EH (I have) and the "What" is in the second word, **tomado** (taken).

Check for Understanding

Using the list of "Basic Actions" from Lesson Eleven, look at the following verbs and try to say <u>what</u> the action is in English and <u>who</u> is doing the action. Do NOT worry about <u>when</u> the action is happening. The point of this exercise is not to learn the endings, but to filter them out so you can guess <u>what</u> is happening. Answers are in the back of the supplemental section.

Examples:

usaron	**What?** <u>use</u>	**Who?**	Ends in –N, so "You all" or "they"
miraríamos	**What?** <u>look</u>	**Who?**	Ends in –MOS, so "we"
tienes	**What?** <u>have</u>	**Who?**	Ends in –S, so intimate "you" (**tú**)
están comiendo	**What?** <u>eat</u>	**Who?**	Ends in –N, so "You all" or "they"
tome	**What?** <u>take</u>	**Who?**	Ends in a vowel, so singular*

*In fact, the verb **tome** may be used with "I," polite "You," and "she" or "he"*

1) necesitará

2) miraba

3) hace

4) ha hablado

5) ponemos

6) usas

7) tomábamos

8) iría

9) escribieron

10) está regresando

11) comen

12) bebí

Help with Understanding WHO

If you understand what action is being talked about, but are unclear as to who is doing (or receiving) the action, you can use one of these expressions to clarify. You can ask **Who?** or **To or For Whom?** You can also use the pronoun as a question (for example, **You???**).

¿Quién?	k'YEHN?	Who?
¿A quién?	ah k'YEHN?	To whom?
¿Para quién?	PAHddah k'YEHN?	For whom?

usted	oo-STETH	You (capitalized in this course to show it is polite)
ustedes	oo-STEH-thehss	You plural (written as You all in this text)
él (note accent mark)	ehl	he
ella	EH-yah	she
ellos	EH-yohs	they*
yo	yoh	I
nosotros	noh-SOH-t'ddohss	we*
para él, ella, ellos, usted, nosotros	PAHddah... etc.	for him, her, them, You, us
para mí (note accent)	PAHddah MEE	(intended) for me

*NOTE: There is also an all-female form of **they** (ellas) and **we** (nosotras).

In this course, you do not actively practice the subject pronouns **he, she, I, they,** or **we** when first learning the essential verbs, because pronouns are not necessary when <u>who</u> is already clear from the verb or the context. For example, there is no need to say <u>yo</u> **tengo** / yoh TEHNG-goh (<u>I</u> have) when **tengo** already means "I have" all by itself. In fact, it sounds conceited to a Spanish speaker if one continually uses the word "I" when it is not required. English speakers tend to overuse subject pronouns in Spanish.

However, **he, she, I, You,** and **they** are sometimes used to emphasize, clarify, or to answer the question **Who?** (¿Quién?). Study the examples on the following page.

Clarifies WHO

No tomó la clase.	(You, s/he) didn't take the class.
¿Quíen?	Who?
Él.	<u>He</u> didn't. ("Him.")

Quisiera ir.	(I, You, s/he) would like to go.
¿Usted?	<u>You</u>?
No, mi amiga.	No, my friend.

Answers WHO?

¿Quién quiere ir?	Who wants to go?
¡Yo!*	<u>I</u> do! ("Me!")
Yo no!*	Not <u>I</u>! ("Not me!")
¡Ella!	<u>She</u> does! ("Her!")

Answers TO or FOR WHOM?

¿Es para ella o para usted?	Is it for <u>her</u> or for <u>You</u>?
Es para mí.*	It's for <u>me</u>.

Le doy el dinero.	I give (You, her, him) the money.
¿A quién?	To whom?
A ella.	To <u>her</u>.

Emphasizes WHO

Pero yo quiero regresar.	But <u>I</u> want to return.

*NOTE: About the Spanish words for "Me"

The word **mí** / mee (with accent mark) meaning "me" is only used after words like **para**, so learn **para mí** (intended for me) as its own, separate expression. The word **mi** / mee (without accent mark) means "my."

With verbs, the English word "me" is usually expressed by the Spanish word **me** / meh (me, to me, myself). For example: **¿Puede dar<u>me</u>...?** (Can You give <u>me</u>?)

When answering a "who" question such as "Who wants to go?" you do NOT answer "me" in Spanish. You answer "I" (yo).

Help with Understanding WHEN

If you understand <u>what</u> action is being talked about, but are unclear as to <u>when</u> the action is, you can ask **When?** or use one of these time expressions as a question (for example, **Now???**)

¿Cuándo?	KWAHN-thoh?	When?
ahora	ah-OHddah	now
en este momento	ehn-EH-s<u>t</u>eh moh-MEHN-<u>t</u>oh	at this time, at this moment
en el pasado	ehn ehl pah-SAH-thoh	in the past
el año pasado	ehl AHN-yoh pah-SAH-thoh	last year
en el futuro	ehn ehl foo-<u>T</u>OOddoh	in the future
en <u>X</u> minutos	ehn <u>X</u> mee-NOO-tohss	in <u>X</u> minutes
hoy	OY	today
ayer	ah-YAIR<i>R</i>	yesterday
mañana	mahn-YAH-nah	tomorrow (or "morning")
más tarde	mahss <u>T</u>AHR<i>R</i>-theh	later ("tarde" also means "afternoon")
antes	AHN-<u>t</u>ehss	before
después	theh-SPWEHss	afterwards
ya	yah	already
nunca	NOONG-cah	never
siempre	s'YEHM-p'ddeh	always

Clarifies WHEN

Mi amigo tomó la clase.
¿Cuándo?
El año pasado.

My friend took the class.
When?
Last year.

Vamos a la tienda.
¿Cuándo?
En quince minutos.

We're going / we go to the store.
When?
In fifteen minutes.

BEEN THERE, DONE THAT:
THE PAST PARTICIPLE

Spanish has several past tenses. Most Spanish grammar classes begin by teaching the preterite tense, which has many irregular verbs, and can only be used to describe <u>completed</u> action in the past. For <u>ongoing</u> or <u>repetitive</u> action, one must use the imperfect tense. There are specific rules which one must learn about when to use the preterite vs. the imperfect tense.

However, the present perfect tense (the verb "to have done" something, plus a past participle) is mostly regular, and is often used in Spanish to describe both completed and ongoing action in the past.

This tense is introduced in Unit Eight (Lesson Sixteen).

Regular Past Participles

The regular past participle corresponds to the –ED or –EN ending after the verb "have" in sentences such as "I have listened" or "He has taken." To make past participles out of regular verbs in Spanish, make these substitutions:

-ADO /AH-thoh for an **-AR** ending

escuchar (to listen to) --> **escuchado** (- listened to)

-IDO / EE-thoh for an **-ER** or **-IR** ending

tener (to have) --> **tenido** (- had)
pedir (to ask for) --> **pedido** (- asked for)

Examples:

He escuchado música.	I have listened to music.
Ha tenido suerte.	You (s/he) have had luck.
Han pedido dinero.	They have asked for money.

NOTE: The past participle is not used by itself in a sentence. It needs to have a conjugated verb. So, although **escuchado** translates as "listened," you cannot say **usted escuchado** (You - listened). You must say **usted ha escuchado** (You <u>have</u> listened.)

Irregular Past Participles

The following verbs (and their derivations) do not fit the regular patterns.

abierto (p.p. of **abrir**)	ah-b'YAIRR-toh	opened (p.p. of to open)
cubierto (p.p. of **cubrir**)	coo-b'YAIRR-toh	covered (p.p. of to cover)
dicho (p.p. of **decir**)	THEE-choh	said (p.p. of to say, to tell)
escrito (p.p. of **escribir**)	eh-sk'DEE-toh	written (p.p. of to write)
hecho (p.p. of **hacer**)	EH-choh	done, made (p.p. of to do)
muerto (p.p. of **morir**)	M'WAIRR-toh	dead (p.p. of to die)
puesto (p.p. of **poner**)	PWEHS-toh	put, set (p.p. of to put)
roto (p.p. of **romper**)	RR OH-toh	broken (p.p. of to break)
visto (p.p. of **ver**)	VEES-toh	seen (p.p. of to see)
vuelto* (p.p. of **volver**)	VWEHL-toh	returned (p.p. of to return)

*You may substitute **regresado** for "returned"

More Uses of the Past Participle

A past participle may be used with the verb "to have done" something: **he** / eh, **ha** / ah, **han** / ahn to talk about the past, or after **está** / eh-STAH to express the state or condition of a person or object. There are also many nouns derived from the past participle.

Examples:

Han puesto el libro allá.   They have set the book over there. (VERB)
La mesa está puesta.   The table is set. (ADJECTIVE)
La puesta del sol es bonita.   The sunset is pretty. (NOUN)

¿Ha practicado usted el vocabulario?

Past Participle as Adjective - Changes to Match Gender (and Number)

When you use the past participle as an adjective, to describe a female or feminine object, you change the –O to –A. And if you are talking about a plural object, you add –S.

Examples:

El lápiz está roto.	The pencil is broken.
La pluma está rota.	The pen is broken.
Los lápices están rotos.	The pencils are broken.
Las plumas están rotas.	The pens are broken.

Past Participle as Verb - Always Ends in -O

When you use the past participle as a verb (after **he** / eh, **ha** / ah, **han** / ahn), the ending is <u>always</u> –O.

Examples:

He roto el lápiz.	I have broken the pencil.
He roto los lápices.	I have broken the pencils.
He roto la pluma.	I have broken the pen.
He roto las plumas.	I have broken the pens.

WAS & WENT

You can use the present perfect tense to talk about most things in the past. However, the following verbs from the preterite tense are very handy. They don't look anything like their present tense forms. Note that **fue** can have two meanings: **was** and **went**. The correct meaning is understood by the context.

fui	fwee	I went (past tense of **voy**)
fue	fweh	You, s/he went (past tense of **va**)
fue	fweh	it was—completed event (past tense of **es**)

MORE "TO ACTION" EXPRESSIONS

You can make sentences using an infinitive, which in English may be described as "to, plus a verb." Examples of infinitives are "to read" (**leer**), "to take" (**tomar**), and "to return" (**regresar**). Infinitives indicate the idea of an action.

If you look up a verb in the dictionary, you will find the infinitive form. It will end in –R (-AR, -ER, or –IR), or –RSE. The **se** / seh is a pronoun that can mean "Your-, him- or her- self." It changes to **me** / meh to say "myself" or "me."

The following expressions all use the infinitive (-R, –RSE, -RME ending). See Lesson Eleven for more information on how to use these constructions.

Please (don't)

Favor de... + infinitive	fah-VOH*RR* theh	Please <u>action</u>
Favor de no... + inf.	fah-VOH*RR* theh NOH	Please don't <u>action</u>

Favor de escribir su nombre.   Please write your name.
Favor de no comer aquí.   Please don't eat here.

It's (not) allowed

Se permite... + inf.	say-pai*rr*-MEE-<u>t</u>eh	It's permitted (allowed) to <u>action</u>
No se permite... + inf.	NOH say-pai*rr*-MEE-<u>t</u>eh	It's not permitted to <u>action</u>

Se permite escribir con lápiz.   It's allowed to write with pencil.
No se permite hablar.   It's not allowed to talk.

Thanks for (not)...

Gracias por... + inf.	g'DAH-s'yahss poh*rr*	Thanks for <u>action</u>(-ing)
Gracias por no... + inf.	g'DAH-s'yahss poh*rr* NOH	Thanks for not <u>action</u>(-ing)

Gracias por escribir.   Thanks for writing.
Gracias por no comer.   Thanks for not eating.

NOTE: **gracias por** can also be used with a noun:

Gracias por su ayuda.   Thanks for (receipt of) your help.

It's time to…

(No) Es hora de… + inf.	(noh) ehss-OHddah theh	It's (not) time <u>to action</u>

Es hora de comer.
No es hora de regresar.

It's time to eat.
It's not time to return.

I like to / I don't like to

Me gusta… + inf.	may GOO-s<u>t</u>ah	I like to (it pleases me) <u>to action</u>
No me gusta… + inf.	noh may GOO-s<u>t</u>ah	I don't like (it doesn't please me) <u>to action</u>

Me gusta comer.
No me gusta ir.

I like (it's pleasing to me) to eat.
I don't like (it's not pleasing) to go.

You, s/he (don't) like to

Le gusta… + inf.	lay GOO-s<u>t</u>ah	You, s/he like to (it pleases) <u>to action</u>
No le gusta… + inf.	noh lay GOO-s<u>t</u>ah	You, s/he don't like to (it pleases) <u>to action</u>

Le gusta beber agua.
No le gusta ir.

You, s/he like, (it pleases) to drink water.
You, s/he don't like (it doesn't please) to go.

It's (not) necessary

(No) Hay que… + inf.	(noh) "AYE" keh	It's (not) necessary <u>to action</u>

Hay que escribir su nombre.
No hay que escribir su nombre.

It's necessary to write your name.
It's not necessary to write your name.

It's (not) good

(No) Es bueno… + inf.	(noh) ehss BWEH-noh	It's (not) good <u>to action</u>

Es bueno comer.
No es bueno comer mucho.

It's good to eat.
It's not good to eat too much.

ESTÁ VS ES: STATE VS. ESSENCE

In English, we use **I am, you are, s/he is,** and **they are** to express various states of being of people and objects, including their location (where they are), their state or condition (how they are), and their "essence" (who or what they are, including name, profession or purpose, and other "essential," or defining, characteristics).

Spanish however, makes a distinction between being in a STATE (location or condition), and being in ESSENCE (name, and "essential" or defining properties).

Spanish also uses the verb "have" (**tengo, tiene, tienen**) in cases in which English would use **am, is, are.** See "When to Be is To Have" in the supplemental section and Unit Five (Lesson Nine) for more information.

STATE of BEING:

estoy	eh-S<u>T</u>OY	I am STATE (location, condition)
está	eh-S<u>T</u>AH	You, s/he, it is STATE (location, condition)
están	eh-S<u>T</u>AHN	You all, they are STATE (location, condition)

Estoy, está, están indicate a STATE of being (location, feeling, condition, appearance). Remember: eSTÁ = STAte.

You will use **estoy, está, están** to talk about <u>where</u> people and things are, <u>how</u> people are <u>feeling</u>, and to describe the <u>condition</u> of things.

Examples:

¿Dónde está el baño?	Where is the bathroom?
Los estudiantes están en la clase.	The students are in the class.
Lo siento, no está.	I'm sorry, s/he is not in.
Estoy bien, gracias.	I'm fine, thanks.
Está bien.	It's fine.
El baño está ocupado.	The bathroom is occupied (busy).

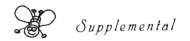
ESSENTIAL CHARACTERISTICS OF BEING:

soy	soy	I am ESSENCE (definition, name)
es	ehss	You s/he, it is ESSENCE (definition, name)
son	sohn	You all, they are ESSENCE (definition, name)

Soy, es, son indicate an ESSENCE of being, or ESSENTIAL characteristics which <u>name</u> or <u>define</u> someone or something. You use **soy, es, son** to tell who or what someone or something is, what a person or thing is <u>like</u> (personality), to say <u>when</u> an event <u>is happening</u>, or to express the <u>time</u>.

Remember: ES-SON = ES-SENce (naming, definition). Also remember: "Time is of the essence."

You will use **soy, es, son** to talk about how things are, as opposed to how they look, feel, or where they've been moved to. You will use **soy** to give your name and job, and **es** or **son** to define or name things or people, to talk about when classes and activities are happening, and to give the date and time.

Examples:

Soy Ana. Soy estudiante.	I'm Ana. I'm (a) student.
¿Qué es? ¿Qué son?	What is it? What are they?
Es un lápiz.	It's a pencil.
El papel es para usted.	The paper is for You.
Es mi hija.	It's my daughter.
La clase es ahora.	The class is today.
La clase es buena.	The class is good.

Ud. es mi amiga.  Estoy muy contenta.

To Be: Permanent or Temporary?

Many textbooks explain that Spanish has two verbs which mean "to be": **ser /
SAIRR** (soy, es, son) and **estar / eh-S̲TAHRR** (estoy, está, están).

The verb **ser** (soy, es, son) is described as being "permanent," while the verb
estar (estoy, está, están) is said to be "temporary. "

This distinction may help you in some cases, but it often becomes confusing if
you don't understand the deeper meanings.

For example, if a houseplant dies, it's **muerta / M'WAIRR-t̲ah** (dead). It's not
coming back. Seems pretty permanent, right? Well, in Spanish you use the
"temporary" verb: **está muerta**. This is because death is seen as a state, not as
an "essential" or defining characteristic of something.

Or, let's say you are a student right now, but you're in the process of finishing
your education and looking for a job. So, being a student is temporary, right?
Well, in Spanish you use the "permanent" verb: **soy estudiante**, because that is
what names or defines you right now. Nothing is really permanent anyway, is it?

The best way to learn to use **ser** (soy, es, son) and **estar** (estoy, está, están) is
to memorize a few concrete examples that you can use right away in
conversation. So, instead of trying to remember that you use **ser** to give your
name, practice saying "I'm…" (**Soy** …) and imagine yourself introducing yourself
to someone. Instead of trying to learn that you use **estar** for feelings and
health, practice "How are You?" (**¿Cómo está?**), and try it out on a friend or co-
worker.

Read about adjectives in the following section and see Unit Five (Lesson Nine)
for more information about **es** and **está**.

ABOUT ADJECTIVES

When nouns change endings, they change meaning. For example, **niño** is boy, **niña** is girl, and **niños** are children.

Spanish adjectives change endings to match a noun, but keep the same meaning. For example, a "busy boy" is a **niño ocupado** / oh-coo-PAH-thoh, a "busy girl" is a **niña ocupada** / oh-coo-PAH-thah, and "busy children" are **niños ocupados** / oh-coo-PAH-thohss. The concept of "busy" doesn't change; only the ending does.

In the dictionary, adjectives are always listed in the "neutral" form, which is the same as the masculine singular. The neutral form can end in –O, -E, -A, or another letter, such as –L.

If the neutral form (adjective in the dictionary) ends in –O, you have to change the –O to –A to talk about something feminine. So, if you looked up "good," you would find **bueno**, but you would have to change it to **buena** to talk about **la niña**.

If the adjective ends in –A, -E, or a consonant in its neutral form, you usually do not change it. Some exceptions are the –DOR ending, which changes to –DORA, and adjectives of nationality like **español** (Spaniard), which changes to **española** (Spanish woman).

Adjectives that end in –E or a consonant don't change to a feminine form, but they still have a plural form. So, with the adjective **interesante** (interesting) you have **niño interesante** and **niña interesante**, but **niños interesantes** and **niñas interesantes**.

Noun-adjective agreement is one of **the most important features** of the Spanish language, yet one of the **last** things for English speakers to master. You will not use many adjectives in this course, so right now it's enough just to **be aware** that this is an important part of Spanish and to start paying attention to endings when you learn new phrases. The rest will come with practice.

Using the wrong ending to describe an object will not usually affect someone's ability to understand you, so for now concentrate on the meanings. When you hear people speaking, however, you will notice that the endings change.

This said, you **do** want to be careful about using adjectives to describe <u>people</u>. For example, if you asked a woman **¿Está ocupado?** (Are you busy?), it would be a bit of an insult, because the –O ending implies that she's a man. Objects such as table and book aren't likely to get offended if you confuse their genders, but a person might.

In Lesson Three, you learn how to describe things using other things (nouns) and a functional word, such as **de** /theh (of, from). Spanish adjectives go DIRECTLY AFTER the main noun. So, "busy bathroom" is **baño ocupado.** There is no need for a functional word in between.

ES vs. ESTÁ with Adjectives

If you make a sentence with an adjective, you might have to decide whether to use **es** or **está.** Sometimes the choice can depend on the perspective and dialect of the speaker. For example, <u>is</u> someone a happy person (definition: **es**) or just <u>feeling</u> happy today (condition: **está**)? <u>Is</u> the object pretty (definition: **es**) or does it <u>look</u> pretty (condition: **está**)?

State or condition:

Está ocupado. / oh-coo-PAH-thoh	It's busy (condition).
Está usado. / oo-SAH-thoh	It's used (condition).
Está bien. / b'YEHN	It's fine (condition).
Está bonito. / boh-NEE-<u>t</u>oh	It looks pretty (condition).
Está contento. / cohn-<u>T</u>EHN-<u>t</u>oh	He's happy (condition).

"Essential" properties or definition:

Es bueno. / BWEH-noh	It's good (by definition).
Es bonito. / boh-NEE-<u>t</u>oh	It's pretty (by definition).
Es barato. / bahDDAH-<u>t</u>oh	It's inexpensive (by definition).
Es feliz. / feh-LEES	He's a happy person (by definition).

KNOW HOW vs. KNOW WHO

Know Something & Know How

There are two ways to say "to know" in Spanish. The first is the verb **saber** / sah-BAIRR, which means "to know a fact, or how to do something." This is a concrete kind of knowledge, and implies you know something completely.

Look at these verbs:

sé	seh	I know (something), I know how to
sabe	SAH-beh	You s/he know (s.t.). know how to
saben	SAH-behn	You all, they know (s.t.), know how to

In this course, you will practice the verb **saber** in the expression "I don't know," (No sé). You will also practice the expression "You know?" (¿Sabe?), which is used as a filler in conversation.

NOTE: The **sé** that means "I know" sounds just like the **se** that means "oneself," but is written with an accent mark. Also, Spanish speakers often use **yo** / yoh (I) or **lo** /loh (it) in front of **saber**. **Yo sé** (<u>I</u> know), **Lo sé** (I know <u>it</u>).

Can: Know How vs. Able To

The verb **saber** can be used with an infinitive to make sentences about things you know (or don't know) how to do. This verb is often used in situations in which an English speaker would use the verb "can."

In Lesson Twelve you learn that Spanish does not make the distinction between something you **can** (are able) and **may** (are permitted) to do. However, Spanish <u>does</u> make a distinction between things you can or can't do because you're able or permitted and things you can or can't do because you know how.

If the ability to do something depends on knowing how to do it, you should use the verb **saber** (to know how).

Examples:

No sé hablar ingles.	noh SAY ah-BLAHRR een-GLEHss	I can't (don't know how) to speak English.
No puedo hablar ingles.	noh PWEH-thoh ah-BLAHRR een-GLEHss	I can't (am not able or permitted) to speak English.
¿Sabe hacer eso?	SAH-bay ah-SAIRR EH-soh?	Can You (do You know how) to do that?
¿Puede hacer eso?	PWEH-theh ah-SAIRR EH-soh?	Can You (are You able or permitted) to do that?

NOTE: When you want to use **sé**, **sabe**, **saben** to mean "know how," you don't need to add in the word "how" (cómo). It's already included in the verb.

Knowing Who (Acquaintance)

The other verb to know, **conocer** / coh-noh-SAIRR , is used for knowing people and places, or having a familiarity with something. The best translation for **conocer** is "to be acquainted with." It can also be used to mean "to meet or visit for the first time." You will not actively use the verb **conocer** in this course.

Look at these examples:

Conozco a su familia.	coh-NOH-skoh ah soo fah-MEEL-yah	I know (to) Your family. (acquaintance)
¿Conoce México?	coh-NOH-seh MEH-hee-coh?	Are You acquainted with Mexico? (visited there)
No conozco ese libro.	noh coh-NOH-skoh EH-seh LEE-b'ddoh	I'm not familiar with that book.
Quiero conocer a su amigo.	k'YEH-ddoh coh-noh-SAIRR ah soo ah-MEE-goh	I want to meet (to) Your friend.

NOTE: You add the word **a** / ah (to) when the action (in this case "knowing" or "meeting") is happening **to** people. Spanish word order is flexible, so the extra "to" (a / ah) helps make it clear who is doing, and who is receiving, the action in a sentence.

WHEN TO BE IS TO HAVE:
TENER EXPRESSIONS

Spanish uses the verb TO HAVE (**tener: tengo, tiene, tienen**) in certain expressions in which English would use TO BE. For example, in Spanish you say, "I have hunger," instead of "I am hungry." Expressions with **tener** / <u>t</u>eh-NAI*RR* (to have, hold, keep) are fairly common in Spanish.

Examples:

Tengo hambre.	TEHNG-goh AHM-b'ddeh	I'm hungry. (have the feeling of hunger)
¿Tiene calor?	<u>T</u>YEH-neh cah-LOH*RR*?	Are You hot? (have the feeling of heat?)

The word used in a **tener** expression doesn't change ending, because it is a noun, just like "book" or "pencil." The book and the pencil do not change their names when different people own them. So, **frío** (the feeling of cold) is the same word whether it is experienced by a man or a woman.

Mi papá tiene frío.	mee pah-PAH <u>T</u>YEH-neh f'ddEE-oh	My dad is cold. (has the feeling of cold)
Mi mamá tiene frío.	mee mah-MAH <u>T</u>YEH-neh f'ddEE-oh	My mom is cold. (has the feeling of cold)

Most of the **tener** expressions are used to describe the physical conditions of living, sentient beings. The verb **estar** (to be in a state: location, condition), on the other hand, is used to describe the physical conditions of both of people and objects.

You would not say **La comida tiene frío**, because that would be like saying "The food is feeling cold."

Instead, you would say **La comida está fría** (The food is cold to the touch).

Remember that the words used with **estar** are adjectives (describing words), while the words used with **tener** are nouns (things).

Nouns used with **tener** don't usually change endings. However, the adjectives used with **estar** DO change endings to match the person or thing they describe.

Examples:

El taco está frío.	ehl TAH-coh eh-STAH f'DDEE-oh	The taco is cold. (to the touch)
La enchilada está fría.	lah ehn-chee-LAH-thah eh-STAH f'DDEE-ah	The enchilada is cold. (to the touch)

NOTE: Usually the noun and related adjective have different forms. For example, **calor** / cah-LOHRR means heat that you feel inside, while **caliente** / cah-L'YEHN-teh means hot to the touch. In the case of **frío** (cold), the noun and the "neutral" form of the adjective look exactly the same.

You will need to learn which conditions are described with **estar**, and which conditions are described with tener. For example, one **is** tired (**está cansado**), but **has** sleepiness (**tiene sueño**).

Examples of things you HAVE, rather than ARE:

tener	teh-NAIRR	to have (for "to be")

frío	f'ddEE-oh	cold (n.)
calor (m.)	cah-LOHRR	heat
hambre (f.)	AHM-b'ddeh	hunger
sed (f.)	seth	thirst
sueño	SWEHN-yoh	sleepiness
suerte (f.)	SWAIRR-teh	luck
miedo	m'YEH-thoh	fear
prisa	p'DDEE-sah	hurriedness
cuidado	kwee-THAH-thoh	care (n.), carefulness
éxito	EHK-see-toh	success
años (m. pl.)	AHN-yohss	years (of age)

NOTE: Be very careful with the pronunciation of **hambre** / AHM-b'ddeh and **años** / AHN-yohss. Also note that the word **años** is special in that it may be used to talk about the age of objects, and it may change to **un año**, if the person or thing is only one year old.

BUENO VS. BIEN

American English speakers sometimes say "good" instead of "well" or "fine" (or use "okay" for everything), so **bueno** and **bien** can be a challenge.

Bueno is an adjective (good), so it is used with a <u>noun</u>. You have already learned **Buenos días, Buenas tardes** (Good day, Good afternoon). "Day" (día) is masculine, and "afternoon" (tarde) is feminine, so the adjective changes form to match the noun. (This only happens with adjectives, <u>not</u> with nouns.) **Bueno** is also used in some expressions in which English might use another word.

El libro es bueno.	The book is good.
La clase es buena.	The class is good.
¡Qué bueno!	Good! Great! How nice!
¿Bueno?	Hello? (Answering the phone-Mexico)
Bueno, pues...	Okay, then...

Notice how you say "es" bueno (buena). Sometimes native speakers use "está" with bueno, to say that someone <u>looks</u> or something <u>tastes</u> good. However, if you want to say someone or something <u>is</u> good, you should say "es" bueno.

Bien, on the other hand, is an adverb (well, fine), and is used with **estoy, está, están**, or an action verb. It never changes its ending.

Estoy bien, gracias.	I'm fine, thanks.
Está bien.	It's fine (it's okay).
No hablo bien el español.	I don't speak Spanish well.

Notice how you say "está" bien. You <u>NEVER</u> say "es" bien when you want to say "It's fine."

¡Usted habla muy
bien el español!

La clase de español
es muy buena.

PARA VS. POR

Look at these words:

para	PAH-ddah	intended for, to, in order to, due by (intended date)

por	POHRR	per, for receipt of, for a PORtion of time or $, by, because

Para and **por** are problematic for English speakers because they can both translate as "for." However, they are each used in very different contexts.

Here are some general guidelines to help you understand their meaning. You will use **para** and **por** in your dialogues, but you will NOT need to memorize the differences to be successful in this course. For now, concentrate on learning examples instead of rules.

"PARA-TROOPER"

Para is a preposition on a mission. Key words for **para** are: intended for, to, in order to, toward a destination, and due by. **Para** represents a specific target, or goal, and may be symbolized by a straight arrow going from point A to point B. If you can use the English "intended for" or "to" to represent the concept, it is appropriate to use **para**.

Examples of para:

clase para niños	class intended for children
papel para escribir	paper intended to write on—paper <u>to</u> write on
teléfono para usted	telephone intended for you—to give <u>to</u> you
para el 6 de mayo	due by May 6 (intended date)
voy para mi casa	going toward home (intended destination)

NOTE: If you want to use a verb after a noun (paper to write, book to read) you <u>must</u> use a preposition. In these examples, you are expressing an intent or intended use of a thing, so you use **para** (intended for, in order to): **papel para escribir, libro para leer.** See Unit Six (Lesson Eleven) for more information.

"POR-TION"

Por on the other hand, can translate as "per," and is used with portions, or amounts of time and money, or to express something done <u>by</u> someone. It is also used in many "fixed" expressions, such as **por favor** (please). It can be symbolized as two lines: one from point A to point B and another from point B to point A. If you can use the English "per," "for receipt of," "in exchange for," "by," or "because" to describe the concept, it is appropriate to use **por.**

Examples of por:

25¢ **por día**	25¢ per day (portion of money)
25¢ **por la leche**	25¢ for the milk (portion & exchange)
por 3 semanas	for three weeks (duration—portion of time)
por la mañana	during the morning (portion of time)
gracias por	thanks for (receipt of something)
por Cervantes	(written) by Cervantes
por aquí	this way (by here)
por eso	because of that (because)
por ejemplo	for example (expression)
por teléfono	on the phone (expression)

Just as with **soy, es, son** and **estoy, está, están,** you are being given general guidelines to help you get started in using these words right away in conversation. There are more uses of **para** and **por** that you will hear, so listen for them and be aware of this. It is not necessary to memorize all the uses at this time. It is more important to begin to develop an intuitive understanding and to be able to use them in contexts that are likely to occur in real life.

Esto es para usted:

¡Gracias por su
participación!

HOW TO USE REFERENCE SHEETS

Several pull-out reference sheets have been created to use with this course text. These are hand-outs with key information condensed onto one page to use alongside the text during class or conversation practice, to serve as a study guide outside class, and to help you communicate with Spanish speakers at work or in other immersion situations.

Visit **www.spanishthatworks.org** to find reference sheets you can print out. Some are free. Others, including various specialty vocabulary reference sheets, are available for purchase.

Alternatively, you may make a copy for your own use of the following pages of the text to use as reference sheets. These are the pages you will most likely want to refer back to as you practice the activities in the course. It is handy to copy them on different colors of paper, so you can locate them quickly when you need them.

"Saying & Understanding Chart" (p. 1-4)
"Social Language" (pp. S-11 to S-15)
"Describing with Nouns- Examples" (p. 2-6)
"Basic Numbers" (pp. 7-4 to 7-5 and p. S-19)
"Basic Things" (p. 1-27)
"Basic Places" (p. 3-11)
"Basic Actions" (p. 6-3)

Plus – The essential (conjugated) verbs introduced throughout the course
Plus – Any specialty vocabulary lists
Plus – "The Spanish Alphabet" (p. S-10), if you need to spell things aloud

HOW TO USE FLASHCARDS

It is helpful to use flashcards to learn the vocabulary in this course, both when studying on your own and when working with a partner. It is fun to use flashcards when you practice the mini-dialogues at the end of each lesson.

How to Prepare Flashcards

Flashcard pages (many for free) that you can print and then cut out with a scissors or paper cutter are available at **www.spanishthatworks.org**. You can also make your own flashcards, using 3 X 5 index cards.

If you make your own flashcards, put the English word or phrase on one side and the Spanish word or phrase as given in the course text *with the pronunciation guide beneath it* on the other side. The purpose of this course is to help you learn *to speak* Spanish, so knowing how to pronounce the words is critical. Be very exact when you copy the information from the course text, so you practice things correctly.

Divide the flashcards into sets, such as "Basic Things" or "Essential Verbs." Secure each set with a small rubber band or a paper clip. You can organize groups of flashcards into ziplock bags.

Using Flashcards to Learn Vocabulary

To study vocabulary, follow the "How to Practice Vocabulary" steps outlined in Lesson Two. The steps are:

1) Rehearsing: Saying & Learning
2) Quiz: Understanding the Spanish
3) Quiz: Saying the Spanish

In order to become fluent in Spanish, you must overlearn the material. This means that you should keep practicing with the flashcards, even when you think you already know them, to improve your pronunciation and speed of recall. It is a good idea to practice a little bit every day, rather than trying to cram a lot of information in at once.

HOW TO USE SENTENCE BUILDERS

Various supplemental hand-outs called "sentence builders" are available via the website (**www.spanishthatworks.org**). The purpose of the sentence builders is to provide additional practice with the vocabulary and structures presented in this course, as well as to teach specialty vocabulary. You can also make your own sentence builders.

How to Make a Sentence Builder

The sentence builders are charts that break down the parts of the sentence into columns, so you can see how everything fits together. They can help you to internalize what you are learning and see how many possibilities for meaning you can create with just a few words and expressions.

To create a sentence builder, lay a piece of paper out horizontally and draw several columns. Each column will contain a certain part speech (noun, verb, etc.) or a word or phrase that complements the sentence (the time an action is happening, a person that an action or object is for, the object of the verb, etc.). You will then list various choices in each column.

For example, to create a simple sentence builder with a two-part verb, you can put conjugated verbs (with any required words) in the first column (**necesito, quiero, tengo que**, etc.), infinitive verbs in the second column (**tomar, comer, leer**, etc.), and various phrases in the third column (**la clase de inglés, un taco con queso, el libro de español, una tarjeta para mi amigo, mañana**, etc.).

How to Use a Sentence Builder

Go from left to right, picking a word or phrase from each column. Continuing the example from above, you could pick **Quiero - leer - el libro de español** (I want - to read – the Spanish book).

In some cases, you may be able (or it may sound better) to omit a word from a column. You may need to apply grammar rules to choose the correct form of a word. (For example, you might need to choose between **el** and **la** to say "the" item.) Remember that a sentence may be a statement or a question, affirmative or negative. Also, you should include a pronunciation guide for any new words.

Practicing with the Sentence Builders

1) Fluency Practice

Read the sentence builder from left to right, choosing words at random. **Don't** think too much about what you are saying. **Do** pay attention to when you have to use the right word in order to make the sentence grammatically correct (such as when you have to choose between **un** or **una**, or **el** or **la**). Use the pronunciation guide to sound out new words.

Sometimes you will make a practical sentence, and sometimes you will make a silly sentence. Whether the sentence is funny or useful, just enjoy it. Concentrate on improving your pronunciation and your ability to making a flowing sentence.

2) Translation Practice

Make sentences, going from left to right. Look at the Spanish words and build from there. Don't think of things that you would like to say in English and then look for the words. Just play with it and see what you can create.

After you have made a sentence, go back and translate it. It may take practice before you can remember exactly what you have just said, but keep trying.

As a variation, you can work with a partner. Partner #1 makes up a sentence, picking words from the sentence builder. Partner #2 translates the sentence.

Partner #1 should just pick the first words that come, without paying too much attention to what they mean. That's Partner #2's job. Sometimes the sentence won't make logical sense, but that's okay. It trains you to listen. Just have fun.

3) Writing Practice

Some people learn well through writing. You may write out the sentences that you create with the sentence builders to reinforce the grammar and vocabulary that you are learning. As a variation, you can work with a partner who must translate what you have written into English.

4) Moving Beyond the Sentence Builders

After you are comfortable with the words on your sentence builders, you may want to use your flashcards or other vocabulary resources to create even more possibilities.

Read about the parts of speech in the "Learning New Vocabulary" section of the supplemental section. Using your flashcards or a dictionary, make lists of nouns (note the gender), and infinitive verbs (-R / -RSE endings). Infinitive verbs are covered in Unit Six (Lesson Eleven).

Go through your sentence builders again, substituting nouns (and infinitives) in the appropriate columns, to come up with brand-new sentences that expand on what you already know.

Let's say that your sentence builder has the word **libro** (book) in a NOUNS column, and the phrase **en español** (in Spanish) in a DESCRIBING column. With this sentence builder, you can create a sentence such as **Tengo un libro en español** (I have a book in Spanish).

Using a dictionary or word list, you can substitute the word **película** (movie) for **libro**, to say **Tengo una película en español** (I have a movie in Spanish).

Or, you can substitute the word **francés** (French) for **español**, and come up with **Tengo un libro en francés** (I have a book in French).

At first, it is best to limit new vocabulary, in order to reinforce basic structures and build fluency. However, once you have mastered a sentence builder, you can apply the same pattern to new words. To continue with our example, you could substitute the word **sombrero** (hat) for **libro**, and improvise the phrase **para la playa** (for the beach), in order to create the sentence **Tengo un sombrero para la playa** (I have a hat for the beach).

Use your imagination, and the possibilities are endless!

"CHECK FOR UNDERSTANDING" ANSWER KEY

The "Check for Understanding" exercises are supposed to be just that—a quick check to see if you understand the procedures or structures that are being explained.

For additional help with pronunciation or vocabulary, listen to the audio program or ask your teacher or another Spanish speaker to help you.

UNIT ONE / Lesson One

The Pronunciation Guide.
Read the words in the pronunciation guide as if they were English nonsense words. The English equivalents of Spanish E, D, R, and T are explained in Lesson One, as well as on the audio program. You will need this information in order to read the pronunciation guide correctly. If possible, have a native speaker listen to you and give you feedback on your pronunciation.

UNIT ONE / Lesson Two

"Things" Words.
Practice your "Things" words, including the "Basic Things" and any specialty vocabulary. Make or use flashcards or study lists.

Read "How to Use Flashcards" in the supplemental section, and "How to Practice Vocabulary" in Unit One (Lesson Two).

Remember that you read the words in the pronunciation guide (below the Spanish) as if they were English nonsense words. If possible, have a native speaker listen to you and give you feedback on your pronunciation.

You may wish to practice the Lesson Two expressions with flashcards before you do the Lesson Two mini-dialogues. You can also listen to the "Basic Customer Service" portion of the audio program.

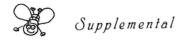

UNIT TWO / Lesson Three

Plurals. 1) Practice making the words on your "Things" flashcards or study lists plural by adding –S, or –ES. Practice the "Basic Things" words, as well as any specialty vocabulary.

"Basic Things" plurals: nombre- nombres, número-números, dirección-direcciones*, libro-libros, trabajo-trabajos, tarjeta-tarjetas, lápiz-lápices** , pluma-plumas, papel-papeles, teléfono-teléfonos, computadora-computadoras, clase-clases.

NOTES
*The accent mark in **dirección** is dropped in **direcciones** because the stress falls naturally on the correct syllable when the word is made plural. Therefore, the written accent is unnecessary.
The spelling change **lápiz-lápices does not affect pronunciation, as "z" and "c" are both pronounced with an "s" sound.

This is a course in speaking, so these special spelling rules will not be actively practiced.

2) Imagine that you are asking if things belong to someone else. Ask "Your (items)?" using the "Things" words, and answer, "Yes, my (items)." If possible, work with a partner. If you are working alone, say both parts. Make sure that you use **sus** and **mis** with the plural words.

"Basic Things" examples: ¿Sus nombres? –Sí, mis nombres, ¿Sus números? –Sí, mis números, ¿Sus direcciones?-Sí, mis direcciones, etc.

Books. Answers will vary. Examples: **libro en inglés** (book in English), **libro en el trabajo** (book at work), **libro para niños** (book for children), **libro por cincuenta centavos** (book for 50 cents), **libro de Ana** (Ana's book), **libro con nombre** (book with name), **libro sin papel** (book without paper), **libro con nombre** (book with name) **libro, papel, y lápiz** (book, paper, and pencil).

Describing Nouns. Answers. 1) trabajo en clase 2) teléfono para usted 3) número de plumas 4) lápiz o pluma 5) trabajo con computadoras 6) lápiz y papel 7) libro sin papel 8) libro de español.

UNIT TWO / Lesson Four

Items. Work with a partner, if possible. If you are working alone, read both parts. Ask and answer if you have various items. Use the "Things" flashcards or study lists you practiced in Lessons Two and Three (including both the "Basic Things" words and any specialty things). You can add plurals and "Describing With Nouns - Examples" from Lesson Three (p. 2-5) if you wish.

Answer the questions "Yes" (Sí) or "No" (No). It is not necessary (and unnecessarily cumbersome) to answer in a complete sentence (Sí, tengo ____, No, no tengo_____, etc.). Just answer **Sí** or **No**. If possible, have a native speaker check your pronunciation of **tengo** and **tiene**.

"Basic Things" examples: ¿Tiene usted nombre?-Sí. ¿Tiene usted dirección?-Sí. ¿Tiene usted número de teléfono?-Sí. ¿Tiene usted computadora en casa?-Sí. ¿Tiene usted libros para niños en su casa?-No.

NOTE: If you are working with a teacher, the teacher may add **un** or **una** ("a") before some of the "Things" words. **Un** and **una** are explained in Lesson Four. Part C. If you are working on your own, or with a partner, just omit the **un** and **una** for now. Native Spanish speakers sometimes drop the word "a" in a question anyway.

Do you have? Work with a partner, asking and answering if you have an elephant, lion, or tiger. If you are working alone, read both parts. Ask the question, and then answer "No, I don't" (No, no tengo).

NOTE: It is not necessary to repeat the vocabulary word back, so DON'T say **No, no tengo elefante, león, tigre.** The only reason that you are saying the verb in the answer is because the Spanish word **no** only means "not" or "don't" when it goes in front of a verb. So, to say "No, I don't," you must say **no** twice: once to mean "no," and once with the the verb (in this case **tengo**), to mean "I don't." Of course, it would also be a correct response just to answer "No."

What is it?
1) Practice saying "a" (**un** or **una**) before the words on your "Things" flashcards or study lists (both the "Basic Things" and any specialty things). Use your flashcards. Work alone or with a partner. If possible, have a native speaker listen to you and correct your pronunciation and grammar.

What is it?, continued

"Basic Things" answers: un nombre, un número, una dirección, un libro, un trabajo, una tarjeta, un lápiz, una pluma, un papel, un teléfono, una computadora, una clase.

2) Practice again, this time with a partner and using flashcards if possible. Ask the question "What is it?" (¿Qué es?). Answer using your basic or specialty "Things" words. Ask and answer the question "What is it?" for each word. Do NOT answer in a complete sentence.

"Basic Things" examples: ¿Qué es?-Un nombre, ¿Qué es?-Un número, ¿Qué es?-Una dirección, ¿Qué es?-Un libro, etc.

NOTE: The plural forms of **un / una** (unos / unas) which translate as "some" in English, are not actively taught in this course. So, if you wish to practice the question "What <u>are</u> they?" **(¿Qué son?** / keh SOHN), just answer with the plural form of the word. For example: ¿Qué son?-Nombres. ¿Qué son?-Números. ¿Qué son?-Direcciones, etc.

UNIT THREE / Lesson Five

Ways to say "the."
1) Practice saying "the" **(el / la)** before the words on your "Things" flashcards or study list (both the "Basic Things" and any specialty things). Work alone or with a partner. If possible, have a native speaker listen to you and correct your pronunciation and grammar.

"Basic Things" answers: el nombre, el número, la dirección, el libro, el trabajo, la tarjeta, el lápiz, la pluma, el papel, el teléfono, la computadora, la clase.

2) Make the "Things" words plural by adding –S or –ES, and practice saying "the" **(los** or **las)** before the words. Work alone or with a partner. If possible, have a native speaker listen to you and correct your pronunciation and grammar.

"Basic Things" answers: los nombres, los números, las direcciones*, los libros, los trabajos, las tarjetas, los lápices**, las plumas, los papeles, los teléfonos, las computadoras, las clases. (See also NOTES on the next page.)

Ways to say "the," continued

NOTES
*The accent mark in **dirección** is dropped in **direcciones** because the stress falls naturally on the correct syllable when the word is made plural. Therefore, the written accent is unnecessary.
The spelling change **lápiz-lápices does not affect pronunciation, as "z" and "c" are both pronounced with an "s" sound.

This is a course in speaking, so these special spelling rules will not be actively practiced.

3) This guessing game is a little like "Go Fish," except there is no pond. Work with a partner. You will need to have your "Things" words on flashcards and on a study list. Follow the model in the text and use the following example as a reference.

Example Guessing-Game Dialogue

1) Partner #1 secretly draws one of the "Things" flashcards.

2) Partner #2 looks at the study list or list in the text and guesses which word might be on Partner #1's card. Partner #2 asks, "Do You have the* …(name from the list)"? **¿Tiene el / la*… (name from the list)?**

3) Partner #1 answers "Yes" (**Sí**) if it's a hit. If it's a miss, Partner #1 says "No," and then tells and shows the correct answer, saying, "I have the*… (name on the card)." **No. *(Pause.)*** **Tengo el / la*** …(name on card).

To make it easier, you can allow three guesses per flashcard. When Partner #1 has finished going through all of his or her flashcards, the partners can switch roles. At the end, the group can compare "hits," or total the "hits" and compare the results to other groups.

NOTES:
*You are saying "the" in the same way you would say, "Do you have <u>the</u> Queen of Spades?"
The pause after the "No" is important because **No tengo WITHOUT the pause means "I <u>don't</u> have." **No. Tengo**…. WITH the pause means "No. I <u>have</u>…"

Here & There

1) **Drill.** Go through your "Things" words ("Basic Things" and any specialty words), using flashcards or a study list. Say both statements for each word.

"Basic Things" examples: El nombre está aquí, Los nombres están allá. El número está aquí, Los números están allá. La dirección está aquí, Las direcciones están allá. La pluma está aquí, Las plumas están allá.

NOTE: The words "here" and "there" don't match singular or plural. This is just a grammar and pronunciation drill to help you build fluency. You are practicing how to plural nouns and verbs and how to stress things on the LAST syllable. If the pens really were <u>here</u> you would say **Las plumas están aquí,** and if the book really were <u>over there</u>, you'd say **El libro está allá.** In the next exercise you will make statements that reflect reality.

2) **Communicate.** Answers will vary. Look around the room and make statements about the locations of things on your flashcards or study lists. Here are some more examples from your "Basic Things" words:

"Basic Things" examples: El libro de español está aquí. La mesa (table) está allá. Las tarjetas están allá. La computadora está allá. Los lápices están aquí.

UNIT THREE / Lesson Six

Places Words.

1) Practice with the flashcards or study list of your "Places" words (both "Basic Places" and any specialty places). Follow the steps outlined in 'How to Practice Vocabulary" in Unit One (Lesson Two).

Read the pronunciation guide (below the Spanish) as if it were English nonsense words. If possible, have a native speaker listen to you and give you feedback on your pronunciation.

2) Practice saying "the" (**el** or **la**) with the basic and specialty "Places" words.

"Basic Places" answers: la entrada, la salida, la sala, el coche, la tienda, la mesa, la oficina, el área*, el piso, el baño, la casa, la calle.

NOTE: The word **área** (f.) is special. Although it is feminine, you say **el** in the singular. So, it is **el** área, but **las** áreas. This is true for some other words starting with an **a** / ah sound, such as agua (f.), which means "water." You say **el agua,** but **las aguas.**

Kinds of Places.

1) Answers: 1) la sala de clase (el salón de clase), 2) el área de computadoras (el área de las computadoras), 3) el baño de mujeres (el baño de las mujeres), 4) la sala 8-B (el salón 8-B), 5) la mesa en la entrada, 6) la sala Lewis & Clark (el salón Lewis & Clark), 7) el baño para hombres (el baño de hombres), 8) la oficina de la señora Padilla.

NOTES: The word for being physically "at" a place is always **en**. The word **a/ ah** in Spanish translates as "at" when used with expressions time ("at two o'clock), but it means "to" a location in Spanish. A native speaker might also describe a "table at the entrance" as **la mesa <u>de</u> la entrada.**

Remember that the word "the" is used more in Spanish than in English. This is something that you can be aware of and listen for as you are learning to speak Spanish. Also. English tends to require or prefer capital letters more than Spanish -for example: **en la calle 8** (on 8th Street).

2) More Combinations. Answers will vary. Rather than thinking of something to say in English and translating to Spanish, make up your own combinations, using your "Places" words and other vocabulary. Then translate to English. Here are some more examples:

"Basic Things & Places" examples: dirección de casa- address of house* (home address), mesa para libros- table for books, papel en la calle**- paper in the street, sala con computadoras- room with computers, trabajo de oficina- office job, clase de computadoras- computer clas, nombre de calle- street name

NOTES: *Remember that you CANNOT put two Spanish nouns together one right after the other. Sometimes the constructions you make with **de** will sound better in English if you put the second noun in front of the first and omit the **de**: "home address" vs. "address of house," etc. **After the word **en** (in, on, at) you may need to say "the" (**el** or **la**) before the next word. You would do this in English as well. For example, "paper in street" does not make sense in English. "Paper in <u>the</u> street" sounds better. It is usually the same in Spanish.

UNIT FOUR / Lesson Seven

Has & Needs. Answers. 1) I need- Necesito 2) They need- Necesitan 3) You have- Usted tiene 4) You all need- Ustedes necesitan 5) She needs- Necesita 6) He has- Tiene 7) The class has- La clase tiene 8) I have- Tengo 9) You all have- Ustedes tienen 10) He needs- Necesita 11) Margarita needs- Margarita necesita 12) They have- Tienen 13) You need- Usted necesita 14) She has- Tiene. (See also NOTES that follow.)

NOTES: The words for "You" and "You all" (You plural) are also not required in Spanish, but they are often used for clarification. The instructions asked you to use **usted / ustedes** in this exercise for the sake of practice.

"The class" (la clase) and "Margarita" use the same verbs as for "he" or "she." You only the need the verb (tiene, necesita) to make a grammatically correct sentence, so if you left off **La clase** or **Margarita**, you didn't do it wrong.

You can find the words for **I, he, she**, and **we** in the "Recognizing Verbs in Other Tenses" portion of the supplemental section. These words are not required in Spanish, and are often overused by English speakers, so for now, you are just learning the essential verbs.

Want, etc. Answers to translation exercise:
1) Quiero un libro en español, por favor. 2) ¿Quiere (usted*) un lápiz? 3) Quieren más. 4) ¿(Ustedes) quieren ayuda?** 5) No quiero nada.*** 6) Mi mamá quiere una pluma.

NOTES:
*Not required, but may add for clarification. You could also say, ¿Usted quiere un lápiz?
**You can say ¿Ustedes quieren ayuda? ¿Quieren ustedes ayuda? or just ¿Quieren ayuda?
***Double negatives are required in Spanish.

2) **Sentences.** Here are some more examples of simple sentences made from the verbs "have," "need," and "want" as presented in Lesson Seven and your "Things" flashcards (basic or specialty).

More "Basic Things" examples: Necesito el teléfono. ¿Quiere una pluma? Tengo más papel. ¿Tiene el libro? Necesita un lápiz. Quiero más, por favor. No tengo la pluma. No necesito nada.* No quiero eso. ¿No necesita su teléfono?

*NOTE: Double negatives are required in Spanish.

UNIT FOUR / Lesson Eight

1) **People Words.** Practice the "Family" words and any specialty people words, using study lists or flashcards. Follow the steps outlined in "How to Practice Vocabulary" in Unit One (Lesson Two).

Read the words in the pronunciation guide (below the Spanish) as if they were English nonsense words. If possible, have a native speaker listen to you and give you feedback on your pronunciation.

2) Translation Exercise. 1) Su mamá necesita un libro. 2) El niño quiere un lápiz. 3) Los estudiantes quieren más. 4) Mis padres necesitan ayuda. 5) Mi papá no necesita nada.* 6) La estudiante quiere una pluma. 7) El estudiante necesita papel. 8) No es mi novio, es mi amigo.

*NOTE: Double negatives are required in Spanish.

UNIT FIVE / Lesson Nine

State or Essence? 1) ESSENCE (name), 2) ESSENCE ("time is of the essence"), 3) STATE (location), 4) STATE (condition), 5) ESSENCE (name, definition, ownership), 6) ESSENCE (defining characteristics), 7) STATE (condition, feeling), 8) STATE (you always say **está bien** to say "it's fine") 9) STATE (location), 10) ESSENCE (defining characteristic, profession).

Translations. 1) Hola, soy Claudia. 2) La junta es ahora. 3) ¿Dónde está Pedro? 4) El señor Padilla está ocupado. 5) ¿Es su hijo? 6) El papel es para la oficina. 7) ¿Cómo está (usted)? 8) Está bien. 9) La señora Smith no está. 10) Soy estudiante*.
*NOTE: You don't usually say "a" with a profession, unless you want to emphasize uniqueness.

UNIT FIVE / Lesson Ten

Phone, please. Answers to translation exercise. 1) Quiero el teléfono, por favor. 2) ¿Tiene (un*) teléfono? 3) ¿Dónde está el teléfono? 4) ¿Hay (un*) teléfono? 5) ¿Me da el teléfono? 6) El teléfono, por favor.
*NOTE: A Spanish speaker might omit the word "a" (**un**) when asking these questions.

Also recommended: Review the verbs in Lesson Seven and the "Social Language" section of the supplemental section (or the "Basic Customer Service" reference sheet) in preparation for the next unit.

UNIT SIX / Lesson Eleven

Actions & More Actions. Practice the "Basic Actions" using flashcards or a study list. Follow the "How to Practice Vocabulary" steps as outlined in Unit One (Lesson Two). Read the words in the pronunciation guide (below the Spanish) as if they were English nonsense words. If possible, have a native speaker listen to you and give you feedback on your pronunciation.

More Actions. Practice any specialty actions words, using flashcards or study lists. Follow the "How to Practice Vocabulary" steps as outlined in Unit One (Lesson Two). Read the words in the pronunciation guide (below the Spanish) as if they were English nonsense words. If possible, have a native speaker listen to you and give you feedback on your pronunciation.

Please Do & Don't. Answers will vary. If possible, have a native speaker check your work. Here are some more examples from the **"Basic Actions"** words:

Favor de. Favor de regresar mañana. Favor de escribir su nombre. Favor de usar el teléfono. Favor de poner sus libros en la mesa. Favor de leer el papel. Favor de ir a la oficina.

Favor de no. Favor de no hablar. Favor de no comer en la sala de las computadoras. Favor de no poner sus papeles allá. Favor de no usar la computadora. Favor de no usar su teléfono aquí.

It's allowed / It's not allowed. Answers will vary. If possible, have a native speaker check your work. Here are some more examples from the **"Basic Actions"** words:

Se permite. Se permite beber agua. Se permite usar el teléfono de la oficina. Se permite comer allá. Se permite usar el libro.

No se permite. No se permite comer en la oficina. No se permite escribir con pluma. No se permite regresar. No se permite hacer eso.

Other Expressions: Examples

Es hora de… Es hora de regresar a casa. No es hora de comer.
Me* gusta… Me* gusta leer. No me* gusta escribir con lápiz.
Le gusta… Le gusta hablar en español. No le gusta ir a la tienda.

See the "To Action Expressions" portion of the supplemental section (p. S-33) for more information and examples.

*NOTE: Be sure to pronounce **me** (to me, me) as "meh" (close to "may"). The word **mi** (my) is pronounced "mee."

UNIT SIX / Lesson Twelve

NOTE about the words for I, he, she, they, and we: These pronouns are not required in Spanish, and are often overused by English speakers, so for now, you are just learning the essential verbs. See "Recognizing Verbs in Other Tenses" on p. S-25 for more information.

Want to / Need to. Answers to translation exercise.
1) ¿Quiere (usted) escribir con pluma? 2) Necesito leer esto. 3) Quieren mirar* el libro. 4) (Usted**) no necesita escribir con pluma. 5) Mi mamá necesita usar el teléfono. 6) ¿(Ustedes**) quieren ir?

NOTES:
*The word "at" is already included in the verb mirar, which can mean "to look <u>at</u>."
**The words for "You" and "You all" (You plural) are not required in Spanish, but they are often used for clarification. You were asked not to use words for "I," "he," "she," or "they."

Have to. Answers to translation exercise.
1) Tiene que escribir con pluma. 2) ¿(Usted*) tiene que usar el teléfono? 3) No tiene que regresar. 4) Tengo que ir a la oficina.

*NOTE: The words for "You" and "You all" (You plural) are not required in Spanish, but they are often used for clarification. You were asked not to use words for "I," "he," "she," or "they."

Sentence Building. For more information about using sentence builders, refer to "How to Use Sentence Builders" (p. S-50 of the supplemental section) or visit the website, **www.spanishthatworks.org**.

Can & May. Answers to translation exercise.
1) ¿Puedo leer esto? 2) (Usted*) puede escribir con pluma.* 3) Mi papa no puede escribir con lápiz. 4) I can't go.

*NOTES: The word for "You" is not required in Spanish, but may be used for clarification. Do not use the word for "I." It is already included in the verb. Also, some native speakers may use the phrase **¿Me permite?** / meh pair*rr*MEE-<u>t</u>eh (Will you permit me?) for ¿May I?.

Let's go. Answers to translation exercise.
1) Vamos a leer esto. 2) Vamos a usar una pluma. 3) Vamos a la junta ahora. 4) Vamos* a la oficina.

*NOTE: You do not need to add an extra "go" in #4—**vamos** is enough. **Vamos a ir a la oficina** would translate into English as "We're going to go to the office."

I'm going to. Answers to translation exercise.
1) Voy a leer esto. 2) ¿(Usted*) va a la clase?** 3) Va a la sala de junta (Va al salón de junta). 4) (Usted*) va a tomar la clase.

NOTES:
*The word for "You" is not required, but may be used for clarification.
**If you wanted to say, "Are you going to go to the class?" you could say, ¿(Usted) va a ir a la clase? However, is not necessary to say "go" twice.

UNIT SEVEN / Lesson Thirteen

Owe & Should. Answers to translation exercise.
1) (Usted*) debe hablar en español. 2) (Usted*) debe cinco centavos. 3) No debo mucho. 4) Debo ir a la junta.

*NOTE: The word for "You" is not required, but may be used for clarification.

How Much?

Ask **¿Cuánto es?** and then say the amount. If you are working on your own, say both parts. Make a study list, obtain the "Numbers, Time, Day, Date" reference sheet (**www.spanishthatworks.org**), or copy pages 7-4 and 7-5 to help you. If possible, have a native speaker check your pronunciation. The numbers are covered on the audio program (see website).

Answers: ¿Cuánto es? $2.10-dos dólares y diez centavos, 25¢-veinte y cinco centavos, $4.45-cuatro dólares y cuarenta y cinco centavos, $1.35-un dólar y treinta y cinco centavos, 90¢-noventa centavos, $8.05-ocho dólares y cinco centavos, 15¢-quince centavos.

NOTE: Speakers from some countries may prefer the one-word spelling for 25 (veinticinco). However, is easier for beginning students to learn one consistent rule for the numbers 16-99.

UNIT SEVEN / Lesson Fourteen

Time. If possible, work with a partner. Ask **¿Qué hora es?** or **¿A qué hora es?** and then give the appropriate response. If you are working on your own, say both parts. Use the "Numbers, Time, Day, Date" reference sheet to help you. Have a native speaker check your pronunciation, if possible.

Answers to "What time is it now?" ¿Qué hora es?: 1:15 - La una y quince*, 9:15 - Las nueve y quince**, 4:10 - Las cuatro y diez, 3:30 - Las tres y media***, 7:50 - Las siete cincuenta****, 8:20 - Las ocho y veinte, 12:05 - Las doce y cinco, 11:10 - Las once y diez.

NOTES: *1:15 - You can also say **La una y cuarto.** **9:15 - You can also say **Las nueve y cuarto.** ***3:30 - It is possible to say **Las tres treinta,** but not common. The word **media** (half) is preferred. ****7:50 - You can also say **Diez para las ocho,** and **Las ocho menos diez.**

Answers to "What time is the meeting?" ¿A qué hora es la junta?: At 1:15 - A la una y quince*, At 9:15 - A las nueve y quince**, At 4:10 - A las cuatro y diez, At 3:30 - A las tres y media***, At 7:50 - A las siete cincuenta****, At 8:20 - A las ocho y veinte, At 12:05 - A las doce y cinco, At 11:10 - A las once y diez.

NOTES: *At 1:15 - You can also say **A la una y cuarto.** **At 9:15 - You can also say **A las nueve y cuarto.** ***At 3:30 - It is possible to say **A las tres treinta,** but not common. The word **media** is preferred. ****At 7:50 - You can say **A diez para las ocho,** and **A las ocho menos diez.** Remember that **a** / ah in Spanish also means "to" a location.

"On" Sunday. Translation exercise.

Answers: el domingo, los martes, el viernes, los lunes y (los) miércoles, el jueves, los sábados y (los) domingos. NOTE: You do not need to say **los** twice.

When?

If you can, work with a partner. If you are working alone, say both parts.

Answers to When? dialogue: ¿Cuándo es la clase de niños? – Los jueves, a las ocho de la mañana. ¿Cuándo es la clase de Internet? - El miércoles, a las nueve y media de la mañana. ¿Cuándo es la clase de computadoras? – Los lunes, a las diez de la mañana. ¿Cuándo es la clase de música? – El sábado, a las dos de la tarde. ¿Cuándo es la clase de inglés? - Los viernes, a las seis y media de la tarde. ¿Cuándo es la clase de español? – Los martes y jueves a las tres de la tarde.

Saying the Date. Answers to translation exercise.
Feb. 17- el diez y siete de febrero, Aug. 3- el tres de agosto, Oct. 22- el veinte y dos de octubre, Jan. 8- el ocho de enero, Mar. 2- el dos de marzo, Jul. 19- el diez y nueve de julio, Jun. 8- el ocho de junio.

UNIT EIGHT / Lesson Fifteen

Names. Answers will vary. Follow the model in the text.

Numbers. Answers will vary. Obtain the "Numbers, Time, Day, Date" reference sheet (**www.spanishthatworks.org**) or copy pages 7-4 and 7-5 to help you with the numbers. Follow the model in the text. If possible, have a native speaker check your pronunciation.

Address. Answers will vary. Obtain the "Numbers, Time, Day, Date" reference sheet (**www.spanishthatworks.org**) or copy pages 7-4 and 7-5 to help you with the numbers. Follow the model in the text. If possible, have a native speaker check your pronunciation.

UNIT EIGHT / Lesson Sixteen

Part of Speech. Answers to exercise. 1) Verb (expresses an action—in this case, an intended action) 2) Noun (it is something you have, even if it is not tangible, and it is used after the word "the," which goes in front of words used as nouns) 3) Adjective (describes the noun "book") 4) Verb (expresses an action—in this case in the past).

Sound check. Answers to exercise: 1) salida / sah-LEE-thah 2) ocupado, ocupada / oh-coo-PAH-thoh, oh-coo-PAH-thah 3) bebida / beh-BEE-thah 4) han hablado / ahn ah-BLAH-thoh (remember the "h" is silent) 5) comida / coh-MEE-thah 6) he comido / eh coh-MEE-thoh.

Been There, Done That. Answers to exercise: 1) beber (to drink)- bebido 2) ocupar (to occupy)- ocupado 3) estar (to be—location, condition)- estado 4) tener (to have, hold, keep)- tenido 5) leer (to read)- leído 6) pedir (to ask for) -pedido 7) tomar (to take)- tomado 8) ser (to be—name, definition)- sido.

NOTE: The accent mark on the "i" in the word **leído** / lay-EE-thoh keeps the "i" from blending with the "e," as happens in the word **veinte** / BANE-teh.

More Past Participles. Answers will vary. Follow the model in the text and check the "Been There, Done That" portion of the supplemental section (p, S-30) for special forms. If possible, have a native speaker check your pronunciation of the words.

Have / Have Not Done. Answers to translation exercise:

1) Su papá ha regresado. 2) Han bebido agua (Han tomado agua). 3) ¿(Usted) ha escrito a su mamá?* 4) No he mirado esto. 5) No he hecho nada. 6) No ha ido a la oficina.

NOTES: The words for "You" and "You all" (You plural) are not required in Spanish, but they are often used for clarification.
*A Spanish speaker might add the pronoun **le** / leh (To him, her, You) to "Have You written to Your mom?" (¿(Usted) le ha escrito a su mamá?) You have not been actively practicing such pronouns in this course, so it is omitted here for sake of simplicity.

Verb or Adjective. Answers to translation exercise.

1) Dad is busy (occupied). 2) Mom is busy (occupied). 3) The bathroom is busy (occupied). 4) The tables are occupied. 5) Dad has occupied the table. 6) Mom has occupied the tables.

Reserve. Answers to translation exercise.

1) I have a reservation. 2) I have reserved the table. 3) I want to reserve a table. 4) The table is reserved.

SUPPLEMENTAL SECTION

Recognizing Verbs in Other Tenses. NOTE: Unless you know all the verb tenses, you will not know if the "singular" verbs would translate as "I," "You, s/he," (or all of these) or the intimate (buddy) you. The complete singular answers are given for your information.

Answers to exercise:
1) necesitará—What? need, Who? singular (You, s/he). 2) miraba—What? look, Who? singular (I, You, s/he). 3) hace—What? do, Who? singular (You, s/he).
4) ha hablado—What? speak (spoken), Who? singular (You, s/he). 5) ponemos—What? put, Who? we. 6) usas—What? use, Who? intimate (buddy) you.
7) tomábamos—What? take, Who? we. 8) iría—What? go, Who? singular (I, You, s/he). 9) escribieron—What? write, Who? You all or they.
10) está regresando—What? return, Who? singular (You, s/he). 11) comen—What? eat, Who? You all or they. 12) bebí—What? drink, Who? singular (I).